GARD

HOLLYWOOD

cendrars sur le bateau
a San Pedro avant son
départ à Hollywood

Jean Guerri

HOLLYWOOD

Mecca *of the* Movies

Blaise Cendrars

with 29 drawings from life by Jean Guérin

translated and introduced by Garrett White

University of California Press

Berkeley • Los Angeles • London

Photo of Blaise Cendrars (p. xviii) reproduced courtesy of
the Swiss Literary Archives, University of Berne.

University of California Press
Berkeley and Los Angeles, California

University of California Press
London, England

Library of Congress Cataloging-in-Publication Data

Cendrars, Blaise, 1887-1961.
    [Hollywood. English]
    Hollywood : mecca of the movies / Blaise Cendrars ; with 29
drawings from life by Jean Guérin ; translated and introduced by
Garrett White.
        p.   cm.
    ISBN 0-520-07807-1 (alk. paper)
    1. Motion pictures—United States—History.   2. Motion picture
industry—California—Los Angeles—History.   I. Title.
PN1993.5.U65C413   1995
384' .8'0979494—dc20   93-37426
                                             CIP

Printed in the United States of America

1 2 3 4 5 6 7 8 9

The paper used in this publication meets the minimum
requirements of American National Standard for Information
Sciences—Permanence of Paper for Printed Library Materials,
ANSI Z39.48–1984. ⊗

Originally published in French as *Hollywood, La Mecque du Cinéma*
by Editions Bernard Grasset, Paris, 1936.

This translation is dedicated to

Contents

List of Drawings

Drawings from life by Jean Guérin

Portrait of Blaise Cendrars *(frontispiece)*

Translator's
Introduction

Blaise Cendrars at Universal Studios
with Edward Arnold, star of the film based
on Cendrars's novel, *Sutter's Gold*.

Les meilleurs films sont ceux que

l'on ne tourne pas ...

Blaise Cendrars, *Bourlinguer*

In 1988, while browsing through the stacks at the UCLA Library in search of Charlie Chaplin's autobiography, I came across a slight volume, misshelved next to Chaplin's book, in a plain brown library binding. Written in pen on the faded spine were two words: *Cendrars — Hollywood*. I opened the book immediately — it hadn't been checked out in years. I could scarcely believe it. Blaise Cendrars, founder, with Apollinaire, Max Jacob, and Pierre Reverdy, of modern French poetry, visionary author of "Easter in New York" and "The Prose of the Trans-Siberian," of *Moravagine*, *Sutter's Gold*, and *Dan Yack*, a powerful presence at the center of the literary and artistic revolution in France before and after the First World War, had come to Hollywood for two weeks in 1936, stayed at the Roosevelt Hotel, and written a book-length article for *Paris-Soir*, one of the largest Parisian dailies of its time.

I hadn't yet read Jay Bochner's *Blaise Cendrars: Discovery and Re-creation*, still the most comprehensive critical work on Cendrars,[1] nor did I know Miriam Cendrars's invaluable biography of her father, first published in 1984.[2] Like many in the United States, I had come to Cendrars belatedly through the *Selected Writings*, published by James Laughlin in 1962[3] at the suggestion of Henry Miller, who for decades — along with John Dos Passos, an early translator of Cendrars[4] — was Cendrars's most eloquent and outspoken advocate in English. I next found a secondhand copy of *Moravagine*, a philosophical revelation of

1. Jay Bochner, *Blaise Cendrars: Discovery and Re-creation* (Toronto: University of Toronto Press, 1978).
2. Miriam Cendrars, *Blaise Cendrars* (Paris: Balland, 1984).
3. Blaise Cendrars, *Selected Writings*, edited and with an introduction by Walter Albert, and translated by Walter Albert, John Dos Passos, and Scott Bates (New York: New Directions, 1962).
4. Blaise Cendrars, *Panama or the Adventures of My Seven Uncles*, translated by John Dos Passos (New York and London: Harper & Brothers, 1931). Includes "The Trans-Siberian," "Panama," and selections from *Kodak* and *Feuilles de route*. Watercolors by Dos Passos.

a madman's violent, nihilistic rampage through Europe and South America from the Russian Revolution through the First World War, and, unbelievably, still the only novel by Cendrars in print by a U.S. publisher (though Peter Owen in England now publishes most of the novels and the four volumes of autobiography). After that reading, my experience with Cendrars was the same as that of a growing number of others, here and abroad: No one who has been touched by the scope of his planetary wanderings, his ecstatic sensibility, his uncanny prescience, can fail to be converted by his art, his overwhelming capacity for life. It is a great pity that, for English-speaking writers who do not read French, Cendrars's *complete works* — in all genres — have been so long out of reach.

Cendrars's writings can be roughly divided into several distinct yet remarkably consistent phases: the poetry, from his Paris debut in 1912 to the mid-twenties, after which he devoted himself to prose (fiction and nonfiction); a period of translation, nonfiction, and reportage that lasted from 1930 to 1940; the years of autobiographical writing from 1943 to 1949; then a last novel (1956) and a growing involvement in radio through the 1950s. The divisions are rough indeed, since many of his works were in progress for years, but they testify to a life of constant motion, and, to use Bochner's term, to the ongoing *re-creation* of the man and the world he interpreted through his art.

For obvious reasons, Cendrars's writing style as a reporter is markedly different from that of his fiction and biographical or autobiographical works. There are syntactical similarities — sentences that go on for entire pages, replete with all manner of digressions, clauses, long lists of verbs and adjectives — but, like any journalist, Cendrars wrote for his audience, adapting theme and style to the publication at hand. And, like any good journalist, he admittedly wrote for money, and for whatever opportunity it may have afforded him to travel. As an illustrated evening paper, *Paris-Soir*'s reputation was built primarily upon entertainment — royal visits, fashion, high society marriages, knowing takes on the day's news, sensational photographs, art, cinema, sports. . . . Thus, *Hollywood* is written in a conversational style, with the confidence of a man reveling in a large popular audience and the tone of a celebrated author and legendary raconteur who could count on being listened to, no matter what he chose to say.

The journalistic context in which Cendrars wrote bears mentioning. The decade of the 1930s was a period of extraordinary growth and change in the French press, and the new trends were perhaps best exemplified in the careers of the renowned journalist and entrepreneur Jean Provoust and his editors Hervé Mille and Pierre Lazareff at *Paris-Soir*.[5] Provoust had taken control of *Paris-Soir* in 1930, at a time when the paper had a daily run of sixty thousand. Under his direction, and later that of Mille and Lazareff, the paper's circulation doubled every year; by the time Cendrars wrote *Hollywood*, it had grown to nearly two million. There were two main reasons for the phenom-

---

5. See *50 Ans de photographie de presse: Archives Photographiques de Paris-Soir, Match, France-Soir* (Paris: Bibliothèque historique de la Ville de Paris, 1990). Catalogue for an exhibition organized by photography critic Thomas Michael Gunther, who discovered these archives in a Parisian warehouse, and Marie de Thézy, conservator of photography at the Bibliothèque Historique.

enal success of *Paris-Soir*, both of which were reflected in editorial trends on the other side of the Atlantic: Prouvost's early understanding of the selling power of the photograph; and his hiring of famous writers not as mere ornaments but as reporters in the field who could bring their subjective talents to bear on a wide range of current events. These included, among many others, Colette, Jean Cocteau, André Maurois, Georges Simenon, Antoine de Saint-Exupéry, and Blaise Cendrars.

The result, at least in Cendrars's case, was a kind of New Journalism far ahead of its time.[6] His first assignment as a reporter had come in 1930 from the weekly *Vu*, for which he immersed himself in the life of Jean Galmot, the famous adventurer, trader, business-

---

6. There has been considerable scholarship on Cendrars the reporter, most of it in French. In addition to the books by Jay Bochner and Miriam Cendrars, see also: Michèle Touret, "Cendrars Reporter," in the special issue of *Sud* (Marseilles, 1988), 133–152, published from the colloquium Modernités de Blaise Cendrars at Cerisy-la-Salle, Normandy, in 1987; and Blaise Cendrars, *Panorama de la pègre et autres reportages* (Paris: Christian Bourgois-10/18, 1986). Compiled by Miriam Cendrars and Pierre Lacassin, and with an extremely helpful preface and bibliography by Lacassin, this latter edition in the "Grands Reporters" pocket series collects most of Cendrars's reportage, with the notable exception of *Rhum*.

man, and diplomat who as a deputy in French Guiana had been an advocate of South American autonomy. Cendrars's research took him to the trial of Galmot's accused poisoners, and the result was *Rhum*, a biographical reportage that says as much about Cendrars the anarchist and solitary adventurer as about his subject. With *Rhum*, Cendrars also followed a pattern he would use for subsequent works of reportage, publishing his writings serially and then later expanding or reworking them in book form. These were not simply compilations, but a way of absorbing what he had done for money and travel into his personal domain. Similar but unfinished books on John Paul Jones and Jim Fisk also date from this period, as does editorial work on life stories of Al Capone and the Swiss con man and adventurer Lieutenant Bringolf. These latter two books were published in a series begun by Cendrars at Editions Au Sans Pareil, titled *Les têtes brûlées*. Cendrars's next newspaper assignments came from the daily *Excelsior* (another *Excelsior* author was Philippe Soupault), for which he wrote a series of documentary reports collected in *Panorama de la pègre* (1935), a detailed exposé on the criminal underworld in Paris, Marseilles, *le pays basque* along the Spanish border, and elsewhere in France. These reports were serialized in April and May of 1934 under the title *Les Gangsters de la Maffia*.

After 1935, Cendrars wrote almost exclusively for *Paris-Soir*. Throughout his journalistic career, he stead-fastly avoided working at a newspaper office — or at any occupation that might have tied him down, for that matter — but seemed to have a particular affinity for the staff at *Paris-Soir*. "Unlike the majority of my colleagues, it was only at the age of fifty, when one is sure of oneself and knows what one has to say, that I started writing for the newspapers, earning my living in total independence, appreciating the team spirit of a newspaper like *Paris-Soir*, but not being part of it."[7]

On May 29, 1935, Cendrars set sail from Le Havre on the maiden voyage of the *Normandie*, a mar-

---

7. Blaise Cendrars, *The Astonished Man*, translated by Nina Rootes (London: Peter Owen, 1970), 153. This is the first of the four volumes of autobiography. "At the age of fifty . . . I started writing for newspapers" — a playfulness with facts typical of Cendrars, since this would have placed the beginning of his journalistic career in 1937.

vel of French engineering and elegance that would set a new transatlantic record to New York on that crossing. Each day, Cendrars broadcast radio messages direct from the *Normandie* to millions of listeners in France, and these were then published serially in *Paris-Soir*. His passionate, detailed praise of this labyrinthine machine — a luxurious, seagoing electrical factory, as he called it — and of the hundreds who operated it, makes of these brief missives an amusing example of journalistic entertainment at its best.

Cendrars's gregariousness, his sense of fun and absolute control of his subject, his outrage or fascination, in *Hollywood* as in other works of reportage, may have belied his true feelings about his tasks as a reporter, but it never showed. In a letter to his mother and siblings concerning his father, Cendrars's son Rémy confided that Cendrars was "bound for New York on the Normandie for *Paris-Soir*, for which he has to write articles in the style of a reporter, something he detests."[8] Nevertheless, he went after

---

8. Miriam Cendrars, *Blaise Cendrars*, 468.

these assignments with extraordinary energy, researching them thoroughly, embellishing here and there to bring to each his personal vision, his penchant for the extreme, and the same subtle, far-reaching erudition and love of life that distinguish all of his poetry and fiction. In January 1936, Pierre Lazareff sent him to Hollywood.

When Blaise Cendrars set out again on the *Normandie* for New York, from which he would travel to Los Angeles by train, he was no stranger to film. He had been among the French avant-garde — Artaud, Cocteau, Desnos, Soupault — who had written rhapsodically about cinema, hailing Chaplin ("Charlot") as a genius and embracing the new medium both in its popular manifestations and as a new form of poetry, a sudden universal language. For several years he envisioned himself as a filmmaker, and was associated at one time or another with, among others, Abel Gance, Jean Epstein, Jean Vigo, Marcel l'Herbier, and Léger (who in *Ballet mécanique* made use of fragments of Cendrars's *La Fin du monde filmée par l'Ange Notre Dame*, the original edition of which Léger had illustrated).[9] Cendrars was apparently vocal enough about these aspirations so that his close friend Léger could write, in a letter to René Clair in March 1923, "This is what I hope for the future: a conception of cinema that finds its own methods. . . . In so far as film continues to be based upon literature and theater, it will amount to nothing. . . . New men like Abel Gance, Blaise Cendrars, and Jean Epstein will be, I hope, the forthcoming directors of this domain which I have only glimpsed."[10]

Cendrars claimed to have worked briefly in a variety of capacities on a documentary series for Pathé titled *La Nature Chez Elle*, but none of this work has ever been recovered. It is known, however, that his first total immersion in film came in collaboration with Abel Gance — director of the classics *J'Accuse* (1919), *La Roue* (1920–1921), and *Napoléon* (1927), and the leading figure in French cinema in the 1920s. In

---

9. Standish D. Lawder, *The Cubist Cinema* (New York: New York University Press, 1975), 84.
10. Philippe Pilard, "Cendrars: Cinéma de rêve, rêve de cinéma," *Sud*, 124.

December 1917, Cendrars arrived in Nice to assist Gance in the production of *J'Accuse*, for which he personally gathered the army of *mutilés de guerre* for the famous final scenes in Part Four, "The Return of the Dead." Having lost his right arm in a battle at the Navarin farm in Champagne while fighting as a *légionnaire* (he was born Swiss), Cendrars himself appears in this sequence, leaning into its star, Séverin Mars, a bandage trailing from his stump.

> On *J'Accuse*, I was everything: workhand, property man, electrician, pyrotechnist, costumer, extra, production manager, aide to the cameraman, assistant director, the boss's driver, bookkeeper, cashier, and in "The Return of the Dead" I played a corpse, all covered in horse blood, for they made me lose my arm a second time for the purposes of the shoot.[11]

---

11. From a 1950 radio interview with Michel Manoll, published in 1952 as *Blaise Cendrars vous parle* by Denoël, and now included in the eight-volume *Oeuvres Complètes* (Paris: Denoël, 1960–1964). This excerpt is from volume 8, p. 673. Manoll's interview is one of the primary sources of information on Cendrars's life. My translation.

It was also Cendrars who recommended that Gance employ his friend Arthur Honegger to write the musical score, a piece later known as *Pacific 231*.

Cendrars's next work for Gance was on *La Roue*. Gance's original title for the film had been *La Rose des rails*, which he changed at Cendrars's suggestion to the more direct, less romantic *La Roue* — the wheel — a symbol, like the locomotive, of modernity and change. This time he worked tirelessly as a full-fledged assistant director, and also assisted in the editing of the film. Consequently, there has been a great deal of speculation concerning the influence of Cendrars's poetry and prose on Gance's fast-cutting techniques in *La Roue*, which in turn influenced Eisenstein's *Potemkin*. Among other testimonies to their complex interaction, Gance's own opinion of Cendrars would seem to support this:

> Our friendship influenced me, as you can see in my book, *Prism*, where I recall in particular my reading, back in 1919, of *Moravagine* in manuscript, and where, on page 313 to be exact, I

wrote his name in third place, after Novalis and Rimbaud, among the poets for whom I have the highest praise. It was Blaise, whose knowledge of esoteric culture was vast, to whom I owe my introduction to Jacob Boehme, who has held an essential place in my thinking.[12]

In fact, many of the dialogue cards for *La Roue* have quotes from Cendrars's poetry, along with quotations from Sophocles, Chamfort, Pascal, Byron, Shelley, Baudelaire, Kipling, Zola, and Claudel, among others. As Richard Abel has written, one of the metaphors current at the time for the art of filmmaking was that of musical orchestration, but another highly articulated and influential view likened film to poetry:

> Although the musical analogy was quite prominent in early French film theory . . . another formulation probably would be more precise — "poetic composition." For the process was similar to that of rhe-

---

12. Abel Gance, "Blaise Cendrars et le cinéma," special Blaise Cendrars issue of *Mercure de France* (Paris, 1962), 170; my translation.

torical and rhythmic patterning in poetry, a kind of
poeticization of the process of representation.[13]

In 1918, while working with Gance on *J'Accuse*,
Cendrars had also begun to formulate his own theories about cinema, elaborated in a series of ecstatic,
almost mystical evocations of the nature of film even-
tually published as *L'ABC du cinéma* in 1926.[14] Although
not collected until years after the making of *La Roue*,
these ideas certainly influenced Gance and what was
then a small community of avant-garde directors,
writers, critics, and theorists. Few writers were more
prophetic. To again quote Richard Abel:

> In . . . *L'ABC du cinéma*, Blaise Cendrars, the idio-
> syncratic poet who had helped Abel Gance shoot

---

13. Richard Abel, *French Cinema: The First Wave, 1915–1929* (Princeton:
Princeton University Press, 1984), 249.
14. Blaise Cendrars, *L'ABC du cinéma* (Paris: Aux Sans Pareil, 1926).
The original French edition of *L'ABC* is currently appended to the
Denoël pocket edition of *La Mecque du cinéma*. An English translation
by Monique Chefdor and Esther Allen has recently been published
by the University of Nebraska as part of a collection of Cendrars's
early short prose, titled *Blaise Cendrars: Modernities and Other Writings*
(Lincoln: University of Nebraska Press, 1992).

and edit *La Roue*, finally published the full text of his essay on the modernity of the cinema. In his elliptical, telegraphic prose style, Cendrars argued that film's fragmentation of reality gave the viewers an intensified experience of the simultaneous flux of life and that the worldwide exhibition of a film created a kind of "global village" of simultaneous audience participation.[15]

Above all, no matter what turns his own career as a filmmaker took, Cendrars never ceased to use the physical medium of filmmaking as a limitless metaphor for the vertiginous movement and hallucinatory rhythm of modern life.

Curiously, if only because his belief in cinema as a supreme art was so profoundly articulate, Cendrars appeared unconcerned with distinctions between high and low art in film and continued to harbor hopes of making quick money as a filmmaker.[16] Even

15. Richard Abel, *French Cinema: The First Wave, 1915–1929*, 261.
16. Philippe Pilard, "Cendrars: Cinéma de rêve, rêve de cinéma," 127.

in *Hollywood*, he seems to criticize the studio system primarily because it had become as venal and bureaucratic as any other big business, but appears just as willing to revel in the popular illusions, in what they represent of the human need to dream, as anyone else. Unfortunately, his own attempts at filmmaking were largely ill-fated. For years he had been collaborating with Jean Cocteau on an ambitious translating and publishing venture at Editions de la Sirène. Shortly after returning from his work with Gance on *La Roue* in the French Alps, Cendrars was informed by Cocteau that Rinascimento Films in Rome was looking for a French director. Cocteau made the necessary arrangements, and Cendrars departed for what turned out to be a year of intense struggle and eventual disaster. His version of the debacle in *The Astonished Man* runs as follows:

> This was in October 1923, on my return from
> Rome, where I had made an important film, *La
> Vénus noire*, starring Dourga, the Hindu dancer
> from the Opéra Comique, and using all the ani-

mals from the zoological gardens, the finest Hagenbeck collection after Hamburg. I had come back broke, victim of the "Banco di Sconto" crash, that international financial scandal carefully mounted by Baron F . . . , who, at the dawn of Mussolini's regime, pocketed all the capital of the Italian film industry, so opportunely amassed during the Great War, and delivered a blow to the industry from which the Italian cinema has never recovered. Personally, I suffered a loss of eight thousand pounds sterling, that is, 1,250,000 francs in round figures . . . the first million I had earned by my work since I had said goodbye, and forever, not to poetry, but to the poets of Paris. . . . And I was back in Paris. Starting from scratch."[17]

Cendrars published the script to *La Vénus noire* during shooting as "La Perle fiévreuse" in *Signaux de France et de Belgique*, serialized in 1921–1922, but the film has been lost, and for decades this story, like so

---

17. Blaise Cendrars, *The Astonished Man*, 122.

many others in Cendrars's fantastic life, had been written off as yet another example of his "mythomania." Thanks to the efforts of Italian scholar Vittorio Martinelli, we now know that the film was indeed made, even reviewed, and received a censor's certificate under the new Mussolini leadership with the title *La Venere nera*.[18] It is quite possible then that, as he claimed, Cendrars destroyed the film himself. Other projects included an unproduced script for Gance, *Les Atlandes*, and a perusal of the script for Jean Vigo's *L'Atalante*.

It is also known that at one time the Brazilian government offered Cendrars several million dollars to write and direct a film on the lives of gauchos, prospectors, Indians, homesteaders — "every kind of adventurer in a country of wide open spaces." This project was interrupted by a coup d'état.[19] Miriam

---

18. Philippe Pilard, "Cendrars: Cinéma de rêve, rêve de cinéma," 125. See also the essay by Alain Masson, "Cendrars, le cinéma et les films," collected in *Blaise Cendrars*, edited by Jean-Marc Debenedetti (Paris: Editions Henri Veyrier, 1985), 139–141.

19. Jérôme Camilly, *Enquête sur l'homme à la main coupée: Blaise Cendrars* (Paris: Le Cherche Midi Éditeur, 1986), 161.

Cendrars also relates that Cendrars once made a proposal to the manager of the story department at Warners, suggesting an ideal continuation of the series begun with Valentino's *The Sheik* and *Son of the Sheik*: a screenplay, to be written by Cendrars, based on a novel he had unearthed, written by none other than Napoléon. Asking price: 250,000 francs.

Cendrars's longest and most complex association with the film industry revolved around the odyssey of the screen adaptation and final production of *L'Or* — *Sutter's Gold* — the story of the Swiss immigrant and millionaire rancher known to all California schoolchildren as John Augustus Sutter. First published by Grasset in 1925, the novel brought Cendrars immediate acclaim, and has since gone through dozens of editions in many languages. In the introduction to her translation, *Complete Postcards from the Americas*,[20] Cendrars scholar Monique Chefdor wrote,

---

20. Blaise Cendrars, *Complete Postcards from the Americas: Poems of the Road and Sea*, translated and with an Introduction by Monique Chefdor (Berkeley, Los Angeles, London: University of California Press, 1976), 20. Contains *Documentaires*, *Feuilles de route*, and *Sud-Américaines*.

Although many previous and subsequent works of Cendrars are more striking in originality and depth, *Sutter's Gold* achieves a kind of perfection in a terse direct blend of imaginative and historical narrative. With his usual empathy for lands and people, Cendrars not only dramatized Sutter's pathetic destiny but turned the California adventure into an allegory of man's destruction through the lure of wealth and technology.

In July 1925, Cendrars wrote to Gance: "There's a great film to be made of *Sutter's Gold*, provided that it is conceived in its entirety and with all of the American technical means available. *It will be a money-maker*."[21]

Despite critical objections to the novel as a travesty of American history, it was serialized successfully in *Cosmopolitan*, and Miriam Cendrars reveals that there was considerable interest in Hollywood in 1926 and 1927 for the screen rights — with one glaring objec-

---

21. Jérôme Camilly, *Enquête sur l'homme à la main coupée*, 157; my translation.

tion: There was no love story.[22] The Famous Players-Lasky Corporation offered a sixty-day option on the book for $1,500, with an eventual purchase price of $15,000. (A note in Ephraim Katz's *Film Encyclopedia* states that Jesse L. Lasky, b. 1880, had been involved in "an abortive adventure as a participant in the Alaska gold rush.")[23] A competing offer arrived from the W. A. Bradley Agency for a thirty-day option at $2,500, with a back-end purchase price of $25,000 and the same stipulation: Where's the love interest? So, in November 1926, Cendrars sat down to work, adding seven pages to make room in Switzerland for the lovely Maria, performer in a traveling circus. The two find each other again in America, then travel north to Vancouver, then south to Idaho and the banks of the Snake River, where Maria meets an untimely death. All Sutter has left is Maria's dog, her constant companion in the circus. Et voilà, on May 16, 1928, Grasset, Harpers, and Cendrars sign a contract with Universal Pictures.

---

22. Miriam Cendrars, *Blaise Cendrars*, 416–421.
23. Ephraim Katz, *The Film Encyclopedia* (New York: Perigree/Putnam, 1982), 692.

It was first announced that William Wyler would direct with John Gilbert in the starring role, but Gilbert couldn't get free of his contract with M.G.M. Then it was revealed that Howard Hawks was slated to direct, and, in fact, Tom Dardis relates in *Some Time in the Sun* that William Faulkner spent most of July 1934 on "an unrealized project of Howard Hawks called *Sutter's Gold*."[24] Perhaps the most intriguing part of the saga occurred in 1929 when Eisenstein traveled to Paris and discussed with Cendrars his ideas for an adaptation of *L'Or* and with James Joyce his ideas for a film version of *Ulysses*. Eisenstein later went to Paramount with his own script for *Sutter's Gold*, based on the Russian translation of the novel by the anarchist Victor Serge, but to no avail.[25] Finally, the film was made at Universal

---

24. Tom Dardis, *Some Time in the Sun: The Hollywood Years of F. Scott Fitzgerald, William Faulkner, Nathanael West, Aldous Huxley, and James Agee* (New York: Charles Scribner's Sons, 1976), 101.

25. Eisenstein's drawings for a shooting script are preserved at the Museum of Modern Art, New York, and have been published by Ivor Montegu, with sketches and text, in *With Eisenstein in Hollywood* (New York: International Publishers, 1967).

with James Cruze (*The Covered Wagon*, 1923) direct-
ing and Edward Arnold and Binnie Barnes in the
starring roles. It was Cruze's 109th film. The governor
of California, Frank Merriam, declared the day of the
world premiere, March 25, 1936, a state holiday, followed by "Sutter's Gold Days" in Sacramento. The
whole concoction was a travesty of Cendrars's original intent in the novel, which he well knew, but when
he later received word of the festivities, he took the
trouble to write to Governor Merriam, stating that it
was high time a statue of Sutter be erected in San
Francisco, and offering to form a Franco-American
committee to finance its construction.

Back in Paris, negotiations were underway for
European distribution of *Sutter's Gold*, when Cendrars learned that another adaptation had been
filmed in Germany without permission and was
about to be released in France. The announcement
read that this film, directed by Luis Trenker under
the title *Der Kaiser von Kalifornien* (The Emperor of
California), had nothing to do with the film currently
underway in Hollywood at Universal with the partic-

ipation of "Greta Garbo, [Charles] Laughton, and other stars, under the direction of William Wyler." Cendrars launched a plagiarism suit — the film was released in France before the Universal version, and included unmistakable "facts" invented by Cendrars in his fictional biography — but without success. At Venice, Trenker's film won the *Coupe Benito Mussolini*, and was praised in Germany by Goebbels.

Production on *Sutter's Gold* was completed at about the time of Cendrars's arrival in Hollywood. He was interviewed by the press, but, as the mere author of a fictional biography, without much fanfare.[26] Cendrars may already have been aware that the film would not be successful; or, perhaps, he simply preferred to travel as soon as possible after completing his assignment. In any case, after two weeks in Hollywood, he chose not to stay for the premiere, boarded the *Wisconsin* in San Pedro Harbor, and returned to Paris — via Mexico, Guatemala, Honduras, the Panama Canal, and the Virgin Islands.

---

26. Miriam Cendrars, *Blaise Cendrars*, 490.

In *Paris-Soir*, meanwhile, the forthcoming *"grand reportage de notre envoyé spécial,"* the famous author and world traveler Blaise Cendrars, had been announced days in advance, and was serialized in the first week of June 1936 under the title *Les Secrets d'Hollywood*.[27] Cendrars revised the text, and *Hollywood: La Mecque du cinéma* was released by Grasset in August 1936. In *Hollywood*, Cendrars could take a good deal for granted with his French audience. European fascination with Hollywood was early and articulate,[28] and there had been a small French colony in the town from its earliest days. As Cendrars knew, no other country had contributed more to photography and cinema than his own, and among the many European pioneers in Hollywood there had been a number of French directors, including Louis Gasnier, Léonce Perret, Emile Chautard, Albert Cappellani, and,

---

27. Michèle Touret, "Cendrars Reporter," 152.
28. For an interesting overview of European involvement in Hollywood from its infancy to the present, see the collection of essays and interviews *Europe-Hollywood et retour*, edited by Michel Boujut with Jules Chancel (Paris: Editions Autrement, 1992).

notably, Maurice Tourneur, many of whom had worked at one time for major French film companies such as Gaumont, Pathé, and Eclair. The most famous Frenchman to have worked in Hollywood in the early years was, of course, Max Linder, the actor and comedian who had inspired Charlie Chaplin.

In 1936, the French colony in Hollywood included Cendrars's friends Robert Florey and Jean Guérin, both of whom he credits with having shown him the city. Florey had come to Hollywood in 1921 as a correspondent for *Cinémagazine*, one of the first movie magazines in France, and quickly distinguished himself as a prolific screenwriter and director with close ties to Hollywood royalty (at one time he had served as director of foreign publicity for Fairbanks, Pickford, and Valentino). Cendrars had known the young painter and illustrator Jean Guérin as a boy in Paris at gatherings at Guérin's mother's house, where Erik Satie often played the piano.[29] At the time, Guérin made his living in Hollywood by

29. Miriam Cendrars, *Blaise Cendrars*, 490.

drawing portraits of stars, and it was apparently Guérin who made the rounds with Cendrars to the studios and to the latest restaurants and clubs, including those on Central Avenue, then one of the hottest jazz scenes outside of Harlem. Perversely, vis-à-vis Hollywood, Cendrars deliberately chose not to publish photographs in his book, preferring instead the simple, witty line drawings by his young friend Guérin, who had often been employed by *Paris-Soir* as an illustrator.[30]

The satiric yet titillating exposé on life in Hollywood by a European writer might well be called a genre of its own.[31] In addition to Florey's early chronicles, there were books by Maurice Leloir (*Cinq mois à Hollywood avec Douglas Fairbanks*, 1929), C. Meunier-Surcouf (*Hollywood au ralenti*, 1929), German novelist Joseph Kessel (*Hollywood, ville mirage*, 1937), Ilya

---

30. Thomas Michael Gunther, "Cinquante ans de photographie de presse," in *50 Ans de photographie de presse*, 48.
31. This point was made recently with an entertaining illustrated chapbook by Christian-Marc Bosséno and Jacques Gerstenkorn, *Hollywood: L'Usine à rêves* (Paris: Gallimard, 1992).

Ehrenburg (*Usine de rêves*, 1939), and René Clair (*Hollywood d'hier et d'aujourd'hui*, 1948), among others, not to mention countless articles in European movie magazines and newspapers on the glamour and depravity of Hollywood. It has often been said by critics, perhaps unfamiliar with the workings of the Hollywood movie industry, that Cendrars's *Hollywood* is a record of closed doors and disappointment. And indeed, Cendrars does confess that the directors and stars he would have loved to meet were "completely booked," and that he was unable to see either Chaplin, Boyer, Lubitsch, or "ace cowboy of the silents" William S. Hart (though he includes a telephone interview of Lubitsch), and goes on at length about the nightmare of gaining entrance to the studios. I believe, however, that these disclaimers should be seen in the light of a very specific journalistic tack, dictated superficially by time constraints but in the main by Cendrars's temperament and notorious dislike of pretense.

Critic Alain Masson raises another interesting question: Who might Cendrars have seen here in 1936, had he taken the time?

To say nothing of those with specifically cinematic talents, here's a Hollywood program that would have pleased him: to drink bourbon with William Faulkner, joke around with Robert Benchley, listen to Oscar Levant play Gershwin, run down Hollywood with F. Scott Fitzgerald, talk about gangsterism with Dashiell Hammett, and speak in praise of journalism with Ben Hecht. He would have been able to spend an evening with the German colony: Bertolt Brecht and Max Reinhardt already counted among the refugees.[32]

Cendrars, of course, could have done that, just as he could have filled his four sprawling autobiographical works with standard literary reminiscences of evenings with Apollinaire, Picasso, Picabia, Robert and Sonia Delaunay, drinking bouts with Léger, Modigliani, or Arthur Cravan — in fact, with portraits of nearly every important writer, painter, or composer before, between, and after the wars. Instead, we find

---

32. Alain Masson, "Cendrars, le cinéma et les films," in *Blaise Cendrars*, 128; my translation.

descriptions of sumptuous meals, endless bottles of great wine, and impossible, otherworldly characters who wander continuously in and out of his solitude — a few famous, most not, and others probably invented. For Cendrars, literature, like film, wasn't something abstract, theoretical — hence his hatred of artistic pretense — it was something *lived*. As he often said, "poetry" — like cinema — "is in the streets."

To put his roadblocks in Hollywood down to bad luck, as some critics have done, and concede that Cendrars simply had to make do as an outsider on a short stay is to overlook the tenor of his other works of reportage, as well as his behavior with regard to the artistic elite of Paris as he had known them. His was always a street-level point of view. "When I go to the United States," Cendrars told Michel Manoll in a 1950 radio interview, "it isn't to meet writers or novelists. I prefer to waste my time on the streets, loaf around with a lad in the midst of washing the windows of a skyscraper and climb with him up to the last floor, then, when evening comes, allow myself to be led by him to Harlem, or some neighborhood music hall or another, or this or that dive."[33] As further evidence of this attitude, during almost the entire four-day crossing of the *Normandie,* Cendrars (who, Miriam Cendrars reports, still didn't own a *smoking*) spent his time in the cavernous engine rooms interviewing the sailors, electricians, laborers, and maintenance engineers who kept the ship running, while Colette, among other celebrity reporters, covered the same voyage from first class. His last report from the *Normandie* recounts a conversation with an engineer who confessed that although the ship utilized the American *rat-proofing system*, in theory one enterprising rat chewing through a certain cable could bring the entire brilliant, luxurious, floating mechanized miracle to a dead stop.[34]

The attraction of Hollywood for Cendrars the world traveler, let alone Cendrars the moviemaker, is understandable. Port cities, trading posts, exotic landscapes, geographical points of convergence for all types of human beings — these were the places in

---

33. Blaise Cendrars, *Blaise Cendrars vous parle,* in *Oeuvres Complètes,* 639; my translation.
34. Blaise Cendrars, *Panorama de la pègre et autres reportages,* 177–179.

which he thrived, the inspiration for much of his work, and the source of the vast experience that enabled him to read the Hollywood scene and skewer it with the glee and displeasure of an estranged insider. In *Hollywood*, he attempted to express what the Dream Factory meant to the average person, to the fans lined up "like the faithful along the approaches to a sanctuary," and from there to draw larger conclusions about the culture as a whole. At work here was a powerful desire to unravel the torrential movement of life not only in Hollywood but in the "totality of the social organism of the United States." At moments, for all its playfulness, his ruminations in *Hollywood* with regard to the proliferation of signs in American culture prefigure those of Barthes and of Baudrilliard. In what might at first seem an early digression, Cendrars explains how a robbery-murder in Manhattan had been hyped and inflated to the proportions of a societal spectacle:

> I quote this random case because it seems to me a typical illustration of the American mentality and gives us a real-life glimpse of the fatal distortion

exerted by illusion on such a grand scale, against a limitless backdrop, inflicting upon the reasoning of man a monstrous complexity, to the point of rendering his logic and his system of simplification and his quality of life absurd.[35]

Or again, referring to the mass migration to Hollywood:

It isn't surprising, you say, to see that all of this is happening in America. . . . But you're forgetting that as America is the land of the fourth dimension, whatever goes on there immediately takes on such proportions that everything becomes vertiginous, and life itself — through the multiplication of a million bits of news and small but very precise details, cut into facets, each reflecting the other into infinity and deluding out of sheer repetition — in no time at all seems to have become unreal, a myth.[36]

---

35. P. 39, below.
36. P. 98, below.

Cendrars's portrayal of Hollywood is amazingly insightful, considering the brevity of his visit, and in many ways as current today as it was then. He arrived in Los Angeles at what is routinely called the height of the studio system, the golden age of Hollywood. This was the year Fritz Lang made his first film here (*Fury*, with Spencer Tracy), the year of William Wyler's *Dodsworth* and *These Three*, of Capra's *Mr. Deeds Goes to Town*, a year featuring dozens of stars from the Hollywood pantheon: Dietrich, Bogart, Harlow, Cooper, Gable, Crawford, Flynn, Barrymore, Stewart, Powell and Loy, Hepburn, Grant . . . As the capital of an industry that had already deluged the world with images, he saw Hollywood as the heart of the Great American Lie, a factory churning out visions of glamour and wealth in the midst of worldwide depression, but for that very reason, a "pole of attraction . . . a touchstone."

Little has changed — not the brutality of the police, not the perennial migration to Los Angeles from other parts of the country and beyond, and certainly not the vanity of producers or the wild hopes of would-be stars. Moviemaking in Hollywood is still a quasi-religious order, closed to the noninitiate unless someone sees an opportunity to make money, and as always thoroughly dependent upon fateful connections. Eager immigrants still hawk star maps from lawn chairs on Sunset Boulevard, and the glittering round of bars, restaurants, and nightclubs where Hollywood goes to see and be seen has gone on more or less the way he knew it for fifty-eight years. He was here for two weeks. He got it right.

GARRETT WHITE
Hollywood, September 1994

For their assistance in the completion of this project I would like to thank David Applefield, Nathalie Bazin, Jean-Pierre Boccara, Jay Bochner, Miriam Cendrars, Brigitte Clément, Albert Friedman, Jackie Gallagher-Lange, Thomas Michael Gunther, Aris Janigian, John Paul Jones [*sic*], Nomi Kleinmuntz, Lisa Magee, Mark Mohler, Michelle Nordon, Judith Trachsel at the Centre d'Etudes Blaise Cendrars, University of Berne, and, above all, Marie-Hélene d'Ovidio at Editions Grasset and Edward Dimendberg at the University of California Press, whose patience and support made this translation possible.

HOLLYWOOD

I dedicate these fleeting pages

TO

PIERRE LAZAREFF

and to his great team at *Paris-Soir*

AND

to my Hollywood friends

FIRST AND FOREMOST

to you, JEAN GUÉRIN, and to you, WALTER SHAW

in whose company I drank day and night

so many good and bad whiskeys

and to you, *Marquise* of Santa Barbara, of Bonair

and other places in the hills

NEXT

to ROBERT FLOREY, to CHARLES BOYER,

to JACQUES THÉRY

who opened up the studios for me

AND FINALLY

to all the city's pretty girls

among them those in my own private *hot jazz* band

KA BALZAC, drum virtuoso

JUNE CRUZE, improviser

TO SAY NOTHING

of KIKI — or MANYA

or Madame La Générale

or La Menteuse,

or CRANEUR, the dog

or MOTUS, the cat

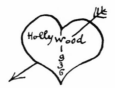

BLAISE CENDRARS

Preface

Well, here it is, my little book about Hollywood. It's certainly incomplete, for in it I say nothing of either my old friend Charlie Chaplin,[1] whom I admire so much, or of Louise Fazenda,[2] the only comic lady of the screen (in France we have Raymone[3] on the stage), the astounding Fazenda, the irresistible Louise, for whom I've had a fancy since the

---

1. Cendrars claimed, in the brief essay, "Charlot," collected in *Trop c'est trop* (Paris: Denoël, 1957), that while working as a juggler in a London music hall around 1909 he had known Chaplin, who according to Cendrars worked the same music hall as a clown. This anecdote is now known, however, to be part of the Cendrars myth.
2. Louise Fazenda, 1895–1962. After 1915, one of the leading female comics with Mack Sennett at Keystone Studios. Fazenda made numerous features in the twenties and thirties, and was married to producer Hal B. Wallis.
3. Raymone Duchateau. First introduced to Cendrars in Paris in 1917, she later became a well-known stage actress as a member of Louis Jouvet's theater company. Raymone was Cendrars's lifelong companion, and his wife after 1949.

days of the silents, neither of directors, nor of the new-
est stars whom I love the most. But having stayed only
two weeks in Hollywood, the directors and the stars
I would have dearly loved to see were completely
booked and had neither the time nor the leisure to
receive me. Louise Fazenda was bringing into the
world — at 42! — her first baby, something I took right
away as a great gag or publicity stunt, but which
turned out to be true, and Charlie was too nervous
when I arrived because he was anticipating the premiere of his latest film,[4] and still too nervous when I
was leaving because it was the day after the premiere,
where he had felt, it was announced on the radio, "as
ill at ease as on the electric chair."

It's also missing a few other things, my book: for
example, portraits of the stars, male and female; a
chapter on the marvelous vanity of producers; a chapter on directors and the hazards of their trade; a chapter on bit players, their ups and downs and their
exploitation; a chapter on the financiers of cinema,

---

4. *Modern Times*, which premiered on February 5, 1936.

those picturesque bohemians of international banking; a chapter on the two thousand writers under contract, attached to the great Hollywood firms, in which
the practice of idleness is the same as in a Tibetan
monastery; a chapter on Walt Disney, that poet of
illusion, whose next film in eight reels, *Snow White and
the Seven Dwarfs*, will require 150,000 animated car-
toons, the perfection of which called for two to three
million rough drafts drawn by hand; a chapter on
color, another on 3-D, the two most recent screen inno-
vations; one chapter on drugs, one on scandals, and
another on divorces, because you'll never understand
anything about the history of Hollywood if you don't
know about the sexual follies that can proliferate in
this hothouse, and how, for example, the murder of
Thelma Todd was a lesbian affair, [5] or how Monsieur

---

5. Thelma Todd, 1905–1935. The source of Cendrars's misinformation
concerning Todd's death is not known, but there is no evidence that
it was a "lesbian affair." An extremely popular comic and dramatic
actress in the late twenties and early thirties, she was found dead in
her car at home, apparently as a result of carbon monoxide poison-
ing. Although ruled a suicide, murder was always suspected and the
exact circumstances of her death remain a mystery.

de Beaugrelon,[6] now settled in California, is in vogue
and the guest of honor at every cocktail party thrown
for him, on the weekend, in every bungalow.

Also missing from my book are the histories of
car thieves and gangsters; an account of the nightclubs, such as the most congenial of all, Louis Prima's
Famous Door, where I met James Wong Howe,[7] the
best cameraman in American filmland (a Chinese!);
or the clamorous Sebastiano's Cotton Club, where
Thompson, masseur to the stars, who looks like a
young corsair and is as beautiful as a fallen angel,

-----

6. No family of the name of Beaugrelon has ever existed in France,
nor apparently does any fictional character of that name appear in
French literature, but a Monsieur de Bougrelon is the main fictional
character of a well-known turn-of-the-century novelette of the same
name by the notoriously homosexual writer Jean Lorrain. This Monsieur de Bougrelon, whose very name suggests homosexuality, is described as a grotesque impostor claiming to be a French aristocrat
living in penurious exile in Amsterdam, and to have at one time
known a glorious past in his native France. This may possibly have
been the source of a mischievous embellishment by Cendrars; if so,
one can only presume that either he or his French publisher misquot-
ed here the name of Lorrain's fictional character.
7. James Wong Howe, 1899-1976. Raised in the United States after
age five, Howe established himself over five decades as one of the
most accomplished cinematographers in Hollywood and was already
well known at the time of Cendrars's visit.

plays the tuba; or Club Alabam, the black nightclub par excellence, where, on Tuesday nights, you can see the housemaids and valets of the stars, in the finery of their bosses, drink, sing, dance, mimic their masters and ostentatiously pass for the kings and queens of the silver screen, and where, every other night of the week, you can hear the most beautiful Southern blues, sung by a mulatto with a captivating voice, sultry features, voluptuous movements, and childlike diction, for whom I wrote an unpublished song, "Mississippi Kisses," which she mouths and burbles ravishingly.

Adrian, the couturier, and Max Factor, the make-up artist, both of them insanely daring, since each of these masters has found a way to rejuvenate his art, a classic art with a venerable tradition, by adapting it to the highly unique proportions and camera angles that, in the special light of the studio or on the big screen, can so easily distort a face or a figure — Adrian and Max Factor also deserved their own chapters. But where would that have led me, good heavens, for one might easily fill a volume of memoirs with the anec-

dotes they could tell — they, who have been established in Hollywood for twenty-five years, who have
known everyone, dressed and hairdressed everyone,
helped all the newcomers, followed every career, witnessed every triumph, and known personally the hab-
its, tics, manias, tastes, adventures, successes, dark
secrets, and intimate disillusions, in short, the fortunes
of the stars, at home as in the studio.

Nevertheless, despite its omissions, I dare to
hope this little book won't disappoint the reader. To
make up for what it lacks, I have the good fortune to
present here the drawings from life by my friend Jean
Guérin, whose pencil is as fast as his eye is mischievous, amused, and faithful, and who has known how
to capture with such exactitude, beneath his seeming
nonchalance — Jean Guérin's drawing is to the drawing of Ingres what stenography is to calligraphy —
some of the most fleeting and most typical aspects of
this astonishing daily improvisation that constitutes
the greatest charm of life in Hollywood, a spectacle
from which you never leave, for in Hollywood, cinema is in the streets.

Indeed, the happiest and most unexpected discovery I made in the capital of photography and the lens was exactly the one made by this young French painter of great talent and exquisite sensibility, this lad who knew how to observe and open an eye, a human eye — and that's why I'm not publishing here a single photograph.

BLAISE CENDRARS

Burgos, September 7, 1936

I

Hollywood, 1936

A Corner on Main Street,
Los Angeles

THE YOUNGEST CAPITAL IN THE WORLD

AND THE CAPITAL OF YOUTH

Streets. Streets. Streets. Streets. There is such confusion, life there is so intense, so diverse, so outlandish, it resembles nothing known.

Hollywood, all at once a bit of Cannes, Coney Island, and Montparnasse, is a marvelous improvisation, a spontaneous, ongoing, permanent performance given day and night in the street against the backdrop of the entire American landscape.

I understand. You either love Hollywood or you hate it. It's a question of age. It's a question of generation. It's practically a question of physiology. "Tell me what condition your arteries are in, and I'll tell you whether or not you should come to Hollywood. . . ." For this faraway suburb of Los Angeles, which has become a world capital in twenty-five years, the industrial capital of cinema, is not only the youngest capital in the world, it's also the capital of youth, a pole of attraction.

That's why for each and every person Hollywood is a touchstone. You either love it or it fills you with horror from the moment you land, from your first step onto its streets.

You can only regret not having come sooner, or, on the contrary, from the simple fact of being there, of having come, of spending one day in such an insouciant and extemporaneous atmosphere, you feel extraordinarily happy. Because you don't see any old people in Hollywood, no more in the studio than on the street. Hollywood is the city of youngsters.

A LUCKY CHARM CITY

To pass through Hollywood on a journey is like knocking on wood: It brings good luck.

And that's exactly what every sailor in the world knows. Hardly a ship drops anchor at San Pedro without half the crew leaping to the ground and storming the miserable taxis, whose drivers, indifferent Mexicans, suddenly roused by the faith, the zeal, the desire of so many young men impatient to visit the last marvel of the world — the illusion factory — speed off and surrender to a vertiginous race down the macadamized road, a straight thirty-mile line that links California's oil port to the mysterious city of the studios, the doors of which are hermetically sealed and the huge glass windows enigmatically made opaque with blue paint.

THE ILLUSION FACTORY

You'll find them stranded in front of the iron gates at every studio, whole crews waiting for an intervention that never occurs.

Not in the least disappointed and like the faithful along the approaches to a sanctuary, the men remain massed there, each one hoping for the chance to glimpse, if only for an instant and from far away, the object of his love or of his secret dream.

Those who lend an ear to the claptrap of the charlatans accosting them end up driving to Beverly Hills under the false pretext of visiting the homes of the most famous stars, and we find them, at night, on the winding canyon roads, every one of them, from the cabin boy to the captain, the victims of phoney guides who have led them to visit places for rent or abandoned houses, and who sell them, before allowing them to go off, souvenirs of Hollywood: Mickey Mouse dolls and toys, Charlie Chaplin's tiny moustache stuck to an elastic string, Greta Garbo's alleged wisdom teeth, Mae West's alleged fingernails in a jewelry box, tufts of hair, unpublished photos, sachets containing a glove, a silk stocking, a flower, each worn by this or that star in such and such a movie — suggestive fetishes these brave sailors carry off to their distant countries as the holy relics of the modern navigator.

MRS. WILCOX, GODMOTHER
OF HOLLYWOOD

To judge by the number of wily hotel touts and petty profiteers who lie in wait for the traveler upon his arrival in Los Angeles and badger him over the phone even in his hotel room, Hollywood must be as frequented a place of pilgrimage as Jerusalem, where the polyglot guides and hawkers of religous trinkets are a plague and follow you even within the Sacred Precincts, down to the tomb of Christ, to offer their often highly dubious services.

But what surprises me about Hollywood is that nowhere, neither in the suitcase nor the hidden pocket-book of the persons who come up to you on the street nor in the windows of the curiosity shops and the stationers, do you catch sight of a single branch of holly, not even on a postcard.

And yet holly ought to be the emblem of Holly-wood, and a bush, a bough, or at the very least a leaf of this plant ought to appear in the coat of arms of this city or in the trademark of every film produced here by the great movie trusts.

I investigated this and, with some difficulty, I finally sorted it out. Mrs. H. H. Wilcox, godmother of Hollywood, had a habit of answering, when asked why she chose the name Hollywood, which refers to the shrub, to christen the lots developed by her husband and that gave birth to the new city,

Beverly Drive

registered under that name in 1903 with a total of 700 inhabitants: "I chose the name Hollywood simply because it sounds nice and because I'm superstitious and holly brings good luck. As you can see, the city is quite successful; unfortunately all of the holly shrubs, which I had brought over at great expense from England and planted along the border of our first subdivision, perished, and I just can't get over it. Despite the success of my husband's enterprise, I'm not at all peaceful, for I love my home and I'm in constant fear of some catastrophe."

Mrs. Wilcox, who must have been a sentimental Englishwoman, died a few years ago, on the eve of the Crash. Today a quiet, out-of-the-way street bears her name, delightfully planted with palms and Japanese pepper trees. In the capital of photography, I couldn't find a single photo or portrait of the godmother of Hollywood, but I was able to come up with a copy of the first document upon which the name Hollywood was written. It's the very map of the "Holly" subdivision. It's dated 1887. I believe it is the oldest known document.

THE "HOLLY" SUBDIVISION

What does this map show us if not streets, streets, streets, streets, a diagram of streets intersecting at right angles between the sea and the mountains?

And it is, by and large, based on this map of the initial subdivision that the city of Hollywood has developed today in a rectangle some thirty miles long and about twelve miles wide.

Note that we also have an image of a house and a château. The house was that of Mrs. Wilcox. It no longer exists, no more than does Prospect, where it stood on its own, for the development's main street became the famous Hollywood Boulevard, universally renowned and one of the noisiest thoroughfares in the world.

MONSIEUR DE LONGPRÉ'S CHÂTEAU

The château was also demolished, but don't go thinking this was an imaginary château. Inquiries made, it was the residence of Monsieur Paul de Longpré, a French painter who had lived here since the beginning of Hollywood, and who passes for having been the founder of the city insofar as a center, a city, of art, and the originator around 1900, if I've understood his role correctly, of the social life, indeed, the fashionable life of this lost corner of far-off California.

THE PRESTIGE OF FRANCE

It's touching, but the thing is so widespread in the United States that we might even ask if it isn't due to some new form of sentimental superstition, of the kind evidenced when the men who cast church bells toss a handful of gold coins as an improving agent into the smelting of the molten bronze: Ever since the age of LaFayette, whose importance and popularity at the time of the War of Independence are known to all, there hasn't been a historical event of any importance in the United States without Americans in one way or another attaching to it, and nine times out of ten it's a complete surprise, the name or the memory of some Frenchman.

This tendency, this national superstition, this precedent by which it seems that the most democratic people on earth have to secure for themselves a kind of title of nobility by latching on to anything French, isn't about to die out in the United States.

Thus, on my previous visit to New York, the press, on the occasion of the opening of the new French church, reported, with a multitude of details, and rejoicing in it heartily as if this little anecdotal fact gave I don't know what glamour and gloss to every child born in New York, that the first two white children born in New York in the colonial period were a little boy and a little girl born to French parents, whose certificates of baptism were discovered during the removal of the archives of the old Huguenot church of the Holy Ghost when it was relocated to 229 East 61st Street.

And so it is that, just like Mrs. Wilcox, Monsieur Paul de Longpré, this French painter whose artistic or social influence is so unclear but who is in the process of becoming legendary in the history of Hollywood, likewise has his own street, a street spelled out *De Longpre Street*, but popularly pronounced *Long-Way Street*, which meant that I had a hell of a time finding it.

It's a well-traveled but sparsely inhabited street with, in its empty lots, cemeteries for automobiles.

HOLLYWOOD TOMORROW
AND 250,000 YEARS AGO

I love Hollywood and I believe in its future and its fortune, not because Hollywood is the universal capital of a new industry in which the roar of money is annually calculated in billions of dollars, but because this city, still in its infancy, is situated, like all cities of art that have played a role in the history of civilization, upon seven hills. In addition to which, as in Florence or Paris, I was awakened each morning by the singing of birds, also a very good sign.

Moreover, we can very well imagine the time — perhaps not so far off as one might think — when not a single studio might still be open in Hollywood, America's young film industry already being strangled by taxation, federal taxes and a tight and complex network of state taxes and social security regulations which strangely compromise its future.

The California movie moguls are perfectly capa-

Santa Monica Beach

ble of closing shop one fine day and of carrying out, without warning, one of the most fantastic financial operations conceivable by transferring their studios to another state, such as Florida, for instance, as there has already been talk of doing. Merely by secretly speculating on the price of real estate, on which the *boom* would then be dizzying in the newly formed capital, they are sure to recoup incredible profits, compensating them a hundredfold both for their present worries and the enormous losses that so stupendous a move of an entire industry would inevitably entail. As shocking as that idea seems at first glance, there is really nothing extravagant about it if one considers that America is the land of radical solutions and thundering financial speculations.

Be that as it may, and even if all the studios were going to close, I would still believe in the future of Hollywood, for the past is the surest guarantee of the future, and hundreds of thousands of years before Mrs. Wilcox gave a name to the region, the area that is now Hollywood was already a perennial center of activity and life. As evidence I need only mention the innumerable skeletons of mammoths gradually disinterred over the last twenty-five years whenever necessary for the building of the present city, all discovered and carried intact to the Los Angeles Museum (which has a much more impressive collection than the Museum of Leningrad) each time ground is broken for a new skyscraper.

Scattered across the planet, there thus exist predestined places where man, since the beginning of time and in the pursuit of great prehistoric herds, has settled, founded a family, and multiplied thanks to his ingenuity and to optimal climatic conditions. These exceptional places of proliferation and life were revealed to man by the prudence of great elephants, very sensitive to variations in temperature and geography. I note, without wanting to make a show of vain erudition, that the early Spanish chronicler Cabrillo pointed out the exuberance of the vegetation and the abundance of game in this valley, and called the climate of the region *deliciosa*, praising in particular the situation of the Cahuanhas Indian villages in the hills "where the mountains begin, well sheltered from the northern winds," at the exact location which today is the site of Hollywood.[8]

Paris, London, Rome, Athens, Peking are all built upon the cemeteries of elephants, and I believe that not one historic metropolis has been able to thrive and endure beyond the area of migration and transhumance of mammoths in the quaternary age, an area thus found to delimit the zone of human civilization.

Hollywood is surrounded by this zone and this is perhaps what best explains its instant success and why it is destined to endure.

Don't imagine that this is some mushroom city on the model of those futureless, ephemeral American settlements abandoned just as soon as they are built because the people there are dying of boredom. Hollywood has managed to occupy and revive an

---

8. As far as I know, no group of American Indians in the Los Angeles area was known as the Cahuanhas. The general term for the indigenous tribes in the Los Angeles region, in use since the late 1800s to refer to Indians living near the San Gabriel Mission, is Gabrielino. However, tribes in the Los Angeles region were traditionally recognized by village, one of the best known of which was Cahuenga, located just over the hill from present-day Hollywood.

ancient center of life where millions upon millions of generations had already come to settle and live in common and rejoice, and it is that long-forgotten past that, despite the new pulsating, improvised, burning character of its streets, makes this city one of the most mysterious and elusive capitals on earth, in a word: a truly forbidden city.

II

The Forbidden City

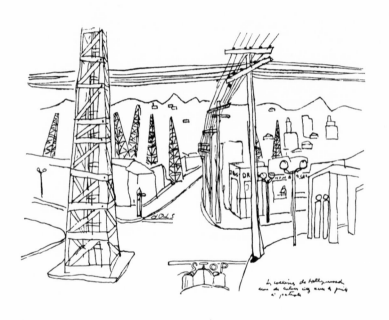

Culver City (M.G.M.)

A NEWS ITEM MAGNIFIED

BY A THOUSAND

A burglar enters a business at night. Thanks to the keys he lifted from the doorman's desk on the way in, he breaks into all sorts of offices. He cracks open desks and file drawers on various floors. Surprised by the night watchman making his rounds, he strikes him down with one shot from his revolver. The police, once informed, search the premises in vain. The murderous thief has disappeared.

Now look, that's a common enough item of news, hardly worth mentioning, and the object at the very most of a scant three-line article in any European newspaper. Well, when I disembarked in New York in January the newspapers were packed with such news, announced on the front page in sensational headlines, to which column after column was devoted for days on end.

TROMPE-L'OEIL, AN AMERICAN
OPTICAL PHENOMENON

If you believe all of that popular hogwash, you've made a big mistake. I'll explain to you how such a thing is possible, and you'll see what it is that magnifies a bit of news by a thousand. In the same stroke, we'll discover one of the greatest American optical phenomena — *trompe-l'oeil*, capable of deceiving reason itself — and you'll understand why Jacques Lory, *Paris-Soir*'s permanent correspondent in Hollywood, calls this city the capital of *the land of the fourth dimension*, a chimerical country discovered by the late Gaston de Pawlowsky, who is remembered as a brilliant chronicler, an inquisitive, witty, waggish, tolerant but often baroque author, a man in the know, an experienced Parisian who wasn't averse to laughing at the things of the New World. That's not such a bad point of view from which to observe American life in all of its often exaggerated, if not hysterical, manifestations, which unfold as in a film and have the look, more often than not, of having been blocked out in advance by a director.

PARADOXES OF FACT AND ACTION

I'll have you know that the building entered by the burgler was none other than the Woolworth Building, one of the most famous skyscrapers in New York; that on his way in the thief had lifted dozens of sets of keys; that he broke into hundreds of offices; that he had already covered I don't know how many floors and reached I don't know what altitude above the level of 5th Avenue when, surprised by the night watchman, he brought the poor guy down with a gunshot before disappearing.

The police, immediately informed, had to mobilize hundreds and hundreds of officers, along with a swarm of detectives, to lay siege to the building, place sentries at all exits, search the skyscraper floor by floor, from the cellars and basements to the top of the building's tower. Nothing less than the methodical exploration of the thousands of offices that comprise the vast cathedral-like edifice, and the opening of tens of thousands of doors and as many unpickable Yale locks (requiring the intervention of a division of locksmiths specialized in security locks), taking four, five, six days. And since they didn't find the man they sought, the operation was recommenced a second and a third time, with the same results, for the culprit had vanished.

Meanwhile, life in this immense commercial beehive came to a complete halt: No one answered the fifty thousand daily phone calls, the radio remained silent, mail wasn't delivered, no transactions were made, and the building's twenty-five thousand employees, unable to enter it to proceed with their work, remained on adjacent streets and were shoved back and held by barricades, mixed with a constantly expanding crowd of the curious flocking from the four corners of the city and bottling up traffic throughout the neighborhood.

Since it was bitterly cold, every bar in the vicinity was jam-packed and stayed that way, overrun since morning by people bantering cheerfully: the drinkers mocking this unusual deployment of police forces joined by firemen sent out with all of their equipment, the loafing bank clerks placing bets on the criminal's chances, and the beautiful typists, exhilarated by an unexpected day of leave with pay, laughing, enjoying themselves, ready to dance, reveling with such fervor that by evening it all took on the appearance of a public holiday, and the entire incident, altogether tragic on account of the death of the night watchman, about whom no one gave another thought, turned to burlesque.

I don't know to what extent they were able to calculate the monetary losses this disturbance of their daily routine, which lasted a good week, imposed on the businessmen whose offices — plush and well equipped to tick off every receipt of money twenty-four hours a day — were in the burglarized building, but I quote this random case because it seems to me a typical illustration of the American mentality and gives us a real-life glimpse of the fatal distortion exerted by illusion on such a grand scale, against a limitless backdrop, inflicting upon the reasoning of man a monstrous complexity, to the point of rendering his logic and his system of simplification and his quality of life absurd.

AMERICA SHOULD REMAIN ASLEEP
FOR TWENTY-FIVE YEARS,
OR ELSE REOPEN ITS BORDERS

The leaders of the United States — in other words, its businessmen — are not, like the statesmen and diplomats of Old Europe after the war (who still have not understood the lightning march of modern times and cling doggedly to the principles and forms of a limping and outdated era), simply unable to keep pace with events, they are above all the victims of their faith in progress and of their own zeal, that is to say, in short, of the perfected technical equipment with which they have endowed their country and the manifold practical accessories with which they have saddled themselves and that encroach upon their lives, even to the depths of their being.

Since the Crash and the slowdown of business, we sometimes have the impression that all of this quasi-automatic machinery is running in neutral and that the American is losing his footing little by little, a bit like the sorcerer's apprentice in the German legend who no longer knew how to stop what he had

Grocery and Bakery

created, an enormous thing that suddenly threatens him, turns to devour him, whose only sin, like that of the American engineer, was an excess of zeal.

Considering the current technical equipment in the United States — which we might call prodigious, luxurious, but also ill-fated, since it goes way beyond the real needs of the nation, making me think that the American economy has leveled off for a more or less long period of time — I personally came to the profound conviction that a new technological revolution that would bring to the country a new era of ease, of wealth, of prosperity, far from preventing the experience of a social revolution, would only on the contrary precipitate a catastrophe that America has courted for some time now.

That is why I am of the opinion that America ought to stabilize and hold its course over at least the next twenty-five years, or else reopen its borders and interest itself a bit more actively in the affairs of Europe, which it has never been able to do.

A country this new and vast, and which is furthermore still in its developing stages, cannot afford to practice the "splendid isolation" of an ancient country.

"FECISTI PATRIAM DIVERSIS

GENTIBUS UNAM"

In 1936, the United States is once again smack in the middle of growing pains, the country is smothering and will soon be out of breath if it keeps to its closed borders, its "quota," the medico-Draconian measures that actually deprive it of the influx, endlessly renewed, of waves of immigrants from every country in the world, of the influx of new blood that in the past gave it its strength and its greatness and without which it wouldn't know how to get by in the future, for lack of which the fever already consuming and exhausting it would rise up to the brain — for one often has the impression today that people in America are going nuts; you really feel that the man on the street or in the country is unbalanced, disappointed, betrayed, spent, leveled and no longer fighting back.

"How many of us are still unemployed?" he asks himself each morning as he opens his newspaper. "Eighteen million? . . . Twenty-eight million? . . . Damn, this is too much!"

So he crumples the paper, and heads for a drink.

A TECHNOCRAT: HAROLD LOEB

I made the foregoing reflections on the train, chatting above a glass of whiskey with my friend Harold Loeb,[9] whom I had met by chance in the dining car of the Chief, the Santa Fe's deluxe train and the fastest express between Chicago and California, known also for its excellent menus, signed by Fred Harvey, greatest chef in the West.

Harold Loeb was on his way to hold conferences in California. I first met him in Rome in 1921, and saw him again in Paris in 1925. At the time he was hanging out with the Dadaists and publishing an international literary magazine, *Broom*, editions of which turned up swaggeringly now in Paris, Rome, London, then in

---

9. Harold Loeb, 1891–1970. A Princeton graduate and son of a wealthy New York broker, Loeb founded *Broom: An International Magazine of the Arts*, which he edited from 1921 to 1924. *Broom* was one of the first English-language journals in Europe and published a great deal of modern French literature in translation, including Cendrars's *Profond aujourd'hui* (Profound Today), translated by Loeb. Loeb wrote several novels in the twenties, but after 1929 devoted himself to work as an economist and government adminstrator. He was famously savaged by his friend Ernest Hemingway, who used him as the model for Robert Cohn in *The Sun Also Rises*.

Berlin, Vienna, Munich or Prague, not out of whimsy, but because at that time the editing moved around according to the exchange rate of the dollar in each of the different European countries.

It was in the magazine *Broom* that Loeb published, among other poetic novelties that ought to have shaken America, a complete English translation of Lautréamont's *Les Chants de Maldoror*, and it's quite a lovely claim to fame for a young American editor, even if the translation (of which he was the coauthor, I believe, with Matthew Josephson)[10] passed by at the time completely unnoticed.

---

10. Matthew Josephson, 1899–1978, expatriate writer and translator, and author of the memoir *Life Among the Surrealists*. In the original French edition of *Hollywood*, Cendrars mistakenly cites the cotranslator as Matthew Jefferson. Actually, it was neither Loeb nor Josephson who translated the excerpts from *Maldoror*, serialized in *Broom*, but the English imagist poet John Rodker. As an editor of *Broom* with Loeb after 1922, Josephson is credited with having introduced many Dada and Surrealist writers to the magazine, and it was Josephson who advised Loeb to publish Rodker's translation. See Harold Loeb, *The Way It Was* (New York: Criterion, 1959); and David E. Shi, *Matthew Josephson, Bourgeois Bohemian* (New Haven and London: Yale University Press, 1981), 52–75.

Harold Loeb's current dada is the reform of the State and this chap Harold today calls himself a "technocrat," since he is the author of the book *The Chart of Plenty* (Viking Press), which was a sensation in official, political, banking, and business circles after Charles Beard, the most eminent contemporary American historian, brought it to public attention as "the most important book of the twentieth century" and the Honorable Byron N. Scott, congressman from California, displayed the book and defended its theme and contents before Congress in Washington in a memorable session on July 1, 1935.

THE AMERICAN CHART OF "PLENTY"

"America must have its fill." Such is — summed up in a single phrase — the program of this book, composed above all of the latest statistics, irrefutable and convincing, bringing to light the following historical fact, namely:

That not only since the collapse of Wall Street in 1929, but furthermore not even during the long period of prosperity that preceded the catastrophe has the

On the Road (Hitchhikers)

potential capacity for production and consumption ever reached its full range of power in the United States.

Now, the yield of this potential could be easily tripled in comparison with the results obtained over the last one hundred years, in all categories and from this day forward, thanks to the electrification of the national machinery that only needs to be intensified, and to the application of a rational plan for the distribution of labor and the redistribution of wealth.

It is therefore necessary, if we sincerely desire to escape the crisis and save the country from the spreading poverty and misery, to triple the capacity of production and consumption in lieu of the desire to reduce it.

America must have its "fill"!

America must forge ahead!

It appears that Harold Loeb's book goes against the theories advocated and the restrictive economic measures applied by the Roosevelt government; nevertheless, this revolutionary work that mercilessly fights the thesis in Washington saw daylight under the aegis of I no longer know what foresight commission in the House of Representatives in Washington, which placed at the disposal of Harold Loeb and his general staff of fifty qualified professors, technicians, economists, and engineers its effective means of investigation and research, its archives, its most secret documents and, for more than a year, the support of its governmental authority and financial aid. *The Chart of Plenty*, it would seem, is practically an official document. Furthermore, the famous statistics published in this book, which lead to the conclusive condemnation and rejection of the capitalist regime, could not have been compiled without the most intimate cooperation of "l'Institute des Finances" — the Brookings Institution of New York (the highest authority on Wall Street!) — which proves and gives us a sense of just how troubled these souls are in America, and how grave the situation there really is.

A FEW STATISTICS, AND TO HELL WITH THE PICTURESQUE!

It takes three days and three nights to go by rail from Chicago to Los Angeles.

I know you shouldn't judge a country in which you've only spent a couple of weeks solely on what you happen to glimpse in a swank hotel lobby or catch from the window of a sleeping car. That is exactly why for me this encounter with Harold Loeb was providential. For three whole days, as the train plunged deeper into the Prairie, a landscape of heartbreaking monotony for the traveler greedy for the unknown, as well as frozen and half-covered with frost at this time of year, I was able to make, thanks to my friend, an unforgettable survey of the horizon, the American picturesque unfolding not at the window of the train that carried us full speed ahead, but directly from our uninterrupted and number-filled conversation.

Thus I was dumbfounded to learn that from 1863 to 1929, in other words, while it was under construction, the national worth of the United States declined by some $600 billion — something which is at the very least unexpected and for the moment remains an inexplicable phenomenon — and that in 1929 the country's gross national product, which should have reached $135 billion had they applied a rational plan, one that would have provided an average of $4,400 as the budget for each American household, barely reached $93 billion, leading to the conclusion that the income of 19 million families fell below $2,500 and that 11 million of these didn't even reach $1,500 in that year.

And since then, the financial situation of each individual has only worsened, for the bungling, the restriction, the mess of production and consumption have reached unimaginable proportions in an era that, like ours, calls itself realistic.

We were able to calculate that from 1929 to 1933 the losses in consumption, due to the noncreation of products, comes to $300 billion — something so extravagant as to be without parallel since there have been people on the planet, people who have given themselves up to industry in order to render this planet habitable, to parcel it out, to live and endure!

America is the richest country on earth. That is an incontestable truth. Great! . . . in this privileged land barely 40% of the population has an income that assures them sufficient means for modern hygiene and decency, and nearly 50% live permanently in con-

ditions just around the corner from poverty. Only 9%
have an income above $5,500 per year, and scarcely 2%
have incomes above $10,000.

IN HOLLYWOOD, ANYONE WHO
WALKS AROUND ON FOOT IS A SUSPECT

When you know these figures, it's hardly surprising
that Hollywood, where some movie people, it would
seem, earn nearly $10,000 in twenty-four hours, should
be a forbidden city, patrolled to the point that anyone
who doesn't drive a car is a suspect!

As a matter of fact, a few days after my arrival,
I was questioned by the police in Hollywood for
walking around there on foot. I confess right away
that it was after midnight — way after. I had had a
lovely evening in the home of a lady, where I had
lingered rather long. Upon leaving, as it was a splendid moonlit night and the hotel wasn't too far way, I
decided to return on foot. I walked down a street
lined with beautiful palm trees, completely happy to
be in Hollywood, not thinking of anything in particular, when a large black car pulled up along the side-

walk and two men jumped out and grabbed me by the arms.

"Your name," they demanded.

"Roosevelt," I replied.

"How's that? Roosevelt?"

"Yes, I'm staying at the Roosevelt Hotel," I said.

"Great!" they said, "but then, what are you doing here?"

"As you can see, " I replied, "I'm taking a walk. The night is beautiful . . ."

"Well, come with us!" and they shoved me into their car and took off double-time to deposit me a few hundred feet ahead at my hotel.

The next morning, when I recounted the incident to friends, they burst out laughing and told me:

"Don't be offended, Cendrars, the same thing happened to Mollison, the English aviator who flew across the Atlantic. Stepping out one evening from a banquet given in his honor by the American Legion at the Victor Hugo restaurant, and deciding like you to return to the Roosevelt on foot, he was stopped by the police and asked to give his name. Having replied that

le masseur
des Stars
Thompson

Thompson, Masseur to the Stars

he was Mollison, the famous aviator, they carted him off to headquarters, the officers supposing to have come across a lunatic, unable to imagine that so famous a man, whose name was all over the newspapers, might be walking the streets on foot like a pauper. . . .

"Consider yourselves lucky, both of you," my friends added, "that the police didn't begin by beating you up!"

"But why?"

"Why?" they asked, bursting out again in laughter, "why, because it never occurs to them that one might walk in a city like Hollywood, where there are more cars than people!"

WILL CALIFORNIA, ESPECIALLY THE CITIES OF LOS ANGELES AND HOLLYWOOD, SURROUND ITSELF WITH A GREAT WALL OF CHINA?

Wouldn't you know that a few days later, as I was being driven along in a car with those same friends, we were stopped on a country road by one, two, three, four barricades of armed police and were unable to go on to make a surprise visit to the great actor William

S. Hart,[11] ace cowboy of the silent era, whom I had hoped to interview at his isolated ranch.

So we turned around, as it was getting late and we thought that the roads must be unsafe. But what was happening? Was there a revolution? Were they tracking baby snatchers through the canyons? No, we had wandered directly into the *blockade* that the California sheriffs and police from several coastal cities like Los Angeles and Hollywood had decided to set up this year along the state border in order to halt the seasonal invasion of the poverty-stricken and the homeless who come from the neighboring states to spend the winter in California and enjoy its mild climate.

Beginning at the end of January, three divisions of police patrolled the border of Oregon, to the north, and of Arizona and Nevada, to the east. Every highway, every footpath was watched, each passage along

---

11. William S. Hart, 1864–1946. Hart's ranch, Hill of the Wind, now William S. Hart Park, is located approximately forty miles north of Los Angeles near the town of Newhall in the Santa Clarita Valley. Ten years after Cendrars's attempt to see Hart, the ranch was willed to the County of Los Angeles as a public park. Hart's home was converted into a museum.

the coast as well as every mountain pass. Checkpoints for questioning and filtering were set up at every place of entry. The approaches to Los Angeles alone were patrolled by 136 officers of the municipal police, placed under the orders of Police Chief Davis, who had assumed responsibility for each one of the measures considered.

Trains were boarded. Vagrants and itinerant agricultural workers were stopped. Families traveling by car were pitilessly forced back if the head of the family didn't have valid reasons to justify his free entry into California. Young people, children, women traveling alone, the jobless, the sick or carriers of germs of infectious diseases were sent back to the states they came from or interned in detention camps under further investigation. Any suspicious individual was arrested and sent to jail.

This blockade had the appearance of a crusade against all undesirables, and the local newspapers, to excuse the harassments, persecutions, and injustices entailed by such exceptional and often exaggerated measures, accuse foreigners, in this case Mexicans who cross the southern border in droves, of coming to eat the bread of the unemployed. But truth obliges me to specify that since the police lines weren't deployed to the south, but directed toward the north and the east, the Californian blockade is certainly directed toward the interior of the country, and 99% of the time the undesirables who were victims of such rigid policies are "foreigners from the interior," that is to say, 100% American, native-born citizens of the states of the east, the midwest and the north — and that's only what I was able to observe with my own eyes, for you know damn well someone's profiting from such a sweet occasion to drive off and send back the masses of the unemployed who arrive from these states. The monstrous roundups and blatant expulsions of Mexicans, on which the California newspapers occasionally report, are only accompanied by this kind of stirring publicity in order to fool the whole country.

A NIGHTTIME HEARING

I was curious enough to sit in on a nighttime hearing before Municipal Judge Scott, who presides perma-

l'orchestre du Cendrars   yvonne guerin

Members of the Jazz Band Cendrars
(June Cruze and Ka Balzac)

nently over the City of Los Angeles. Seventy-eight men who had been arrested during the day filed hastily past him. Of these, ten young men who swore on the Bible to get out of town and leave California within forty-eight hours were released immediately. Sixty were sentenced to ten days in jail, twenty-eight of whom were criminals originally from the east and upon whose passing one had to ask a few additional questions, the others being unfortunates who were caught hopping freight trains — *hobos*,[12] as they call them over there. Only eight were cleared of all charges. As it turned out that night, of the seventy-eight undesirables who filed past Judge Scott, there wasn't a single foreigner, probably because I was there incognito, yours truly, a foreign journalist.

CAN THE HILLBILLIES BE KEPT FROM COMING TO SEEK THEIR FORTUNES IN . . . HOLLYWOOD?

I was even curious enough to question as they were leaving the eight men who were declared innocent,

---

12. In the original French edition, this word was printed as *bobos*.

and, a short while later, to buy drinks and meals for the ten young men who had been released on parole. These men and youngsters had come to California in perfectly good faith in search of a job. One of them had even worked for eight days as a carpenter in a Hollywood studio. They all came from humble circumstances, certainly, but not one of them was homeless or a beggar. If anything, they were saddened by the adventure, and ashamed of having come just to bash their heads against the blockade.

Can the hillbillies from the interior be kept from coming to seek their fortunes in . . . Hollywood?

When will they build their Chinese wall?

But the fact is, the wall exists, it surrounds the studios, in the heart of the city.

THE UTOPIA OF HORSEPOWER

His book on the table, skimming through the statistics, talking numbers, juggling them perhaps, but, and this I swear, never falling back on dialectical trickery, no more to condemn the regime than to try to convince me of the superiority of his thesis, because deep down he knew I was skeptical on more than one point, above all when he took to talking about the future, Harold Loeb — who is not a Marxist but rather calls himself a "technocrat," a committed believer whose conception of future society is neither proletarian, nor authoritarian, nor fascist, but rests upon the American democratic tradition and more closely resembles a scientific cooperation of labor, in which each of the participants would have a right to the riches created and to a certain standard of living and comfort according to their professional collaboration, rather than full-fledged communism — outlined for me a bleak picture of his country's economic depression and enumerated, with stubborn, cold conviction, yet not without sympathy even though he never let go the exclusive point of view of the engineer, every profound moral and material transformation he anticipated from the strict application of his plan, for whose promotion and popularization, moreover, he had undertaken to travel, invited by the great universities and open discussion clubs, which are innumerable in the United States.

Up to this point I had been following Harold

attentively, but when he began talking about the future, the abolition of poverty, disease, misfortune, evil, I confess that I suddenly lost interest.

Ever since it was published, the Soviet Five-Year Plan has spawned so many offshoots around the world that each time I hear one of these "horsepower" prophets exposing in front of me his reform plan that will guarantee the happiness of all citizens, I have a mind to shout, "So just let the Soviets work in peace! We'll see soon enough if the comrade engineers will be able to clean from their gears the ancient human perversity that warps, outwits all calculations! The rest of you good people, Christians of the West, hold your tongues! or else, if you really want to make a fresh start and surrender yourselves to a new experience, start by doing away with work, that curse mentioned so long ago in the Bible! . . ." Because it seems to me that the problem is misplaced, and that it is not so much work as man's leisure that is in urgent need of organization,[13] the lei-

---

13. *Author's Note:* I had no idea while writing this that less than a month later (June 1936) the Blum cabinet was going to offer us in France leisure activities organized by order of the Ministry! . . . B.C.

sure hours to which we owe art, love, the invention of writing, et cetera, in short, everything that helps to sustain our lives. Man does not live by bread alone — and it is that truth that has been lost today.

THE PRIME IMPORTANCE
OF TODAY'S REALITY

I never take notes when I travel. I don't want to clutter my mind with a multitude of contradictory details. I want to be able to report only the essential in what I see.

A reporter is not a mere image hunter, he must know how to capture views of the mind.

If his eye is to be as fast as the photographer's lens, his role is not to passively record things. The spirit of the author must react with agility, his writer's temperament, his human heart.

It is in this way, and in this way only, that a reportage can be a sensational document, and not through exaggerations.

Nothing is as thrilling for an investigative reporter who has just set out incognito for a foreign country than to retrieve from that plunge a living, pulsating, rebellious present, yet of general interest and the only real testimony we may be able to give of that unknown, the life of the universe. That's why newspapers exist, and why they're published every twenty-four hours.

It's not a question of being objective. You've got to take sides. Without involving something of himself, a journalist will never find a way to render this present life, which is also a vision of the mind.

Therefore, the truer a "report," the more imaginary it will appear; to stay close to the truth, it must soak into things and color them rather than simply trace their outlines. And that is also why writing is neither a lie, nor a dream, but reality, and perhaps all we may ever know of the real.

FROM THE CIRCUIT OF ADOBE
TRAIN STATIONS TO THE MOVABLE
SCENES OF PRINCE POTEMKIN

Don't think I'm exaggerating. As Loeb, this lad of reason so completely stuffed with numbers, began to talk about the future, the train was crossing the legendary land of New Mexico, and my spirit was strangely trou-

marlene Dietrich

tournant avec Boyer

" y love the Soldier "

Marlene Dietrich

bled, both by the visions of distant tomorrows my companion was reeling out and because my eye was unconsciously taking in through the train window something of the desert and the solitudes we were passing through.

It was the morning of the third day. Several times already the train had stopped at one of these immense adobe train stations, station-hotels, empty but decorative, built, according to local tradition, of kneaded earth, and in the old Mexican colonial style that Fred Harvey, who is not only the greatest cook in the West but also its very modern manager, had built here and there from Texas to Arizona in order to attract tourists — a goal that obliged him to furnish — in truth, to disguise — the Prairie. For, behind these cumbersome stations, behind these imitation architectures, nine times out of ten there is nothing, not one hamlet, not one village.

I have no idea by what bizarre whimsy a correlation had formed in my mind between my friend's quasi-mathematical deductions and these brand-new but absurd buildings.

I had a feeling of déjà vu, of having heard this before, of a mistake, or a lie.

"It's just a *bluff*," I thought to myself, "an American *bluff*..."

But I wasn't happy with this explanation, and I searched for what these words, these buildings, reminded me of, what they hid from me.

Several times that day I thought I had found what was bothering me, but, thanks to fatigue, as well as the swaying of the train and the monotony of the voyage, I couldn't quite grasp the reason for my unease.

"Now look," I said to myself, staring absentmindedly at a landscape that hadn't changed since Chicago, which is to say, a barren landscape in which there wasn't exactly nothing, but nothing you could follow with your eyes. "Look, we can't condemn the one to justify the other, since capitalism and communism are flip sides of the same question and one doesn't work without the other. . . . What amazes me is that while we've been talking about all of these beautiful dreams benumeraled with a better distribution of wealth and a finer exploitation of the planet, none of them have been realized! . . . Human misery. . . . I'm sure that each one of these ideologues is sincere and right in his own way; but I'm just as sure and certain that none of it is going to happen the way any of them thinks it will, because even if the economy submits to harsh measures, life is not logical, nature isn't just going to roll over — and that's why man is powerless and can't predict anything, since his destiny is not the end, either of life or of nature. . . . *That* is scientific reasoning. . . . How then can we go on giving ourselves up to the illusion of an expired ideology? All of these current figures and all of the 'horsepower' in the modern world won't change a thing about the march of business and the destiny of man. . . . When engineers in their turn become prophets and wander into delirium, they manufacture nothing but utopia. . . . Dialectical materialism is old-fashioned . . . it's precisely for having listened too much and followed too much, and, alas! for having tried way too hard to put theories into practice, disinterestedly, of course, but how many crazy ones there have been (it seems to me that today we've already paid dearly enough to find out!) from philosophers and economists of the eighteenth century, those nonspecialist savants, *friends of the human race* as they liked to call themselves while addressing not only their own countries, like my American 'technocrat' or Stalin, but all the peoples of the earth, that the world today is struggling at the bottom of the blender into which it has fallen. . . ."

Loeb is Jewish.[14] He comes from a family of industrialists with huge interests in the steel mills of Bethlehem (Pennsylvania). He has a scientific background. When he came over to rub shoulders with Dada, he basically came to blow off a little steam. Of his association with the Aragons and Bretons, all that's left is a profound contempt for poetry and literature. And nevertheless, it is these figures that have moved

------

14. It is perhaps necessary to point out that, taken in context, Cendrars's mention of Loeb's Jewishness need not be interpreted as anti-Semitic. He introduces Loeb as his friend, and praises his work as an avant-garde publisher. As elsewhere, it was customary for Cendrars to place his subjects according to background. At issue in these passages is Cendrars's distrust of any kind of programmatic utopianism, whether from the left or the right. It perhaps also bears mentioning that Cendrars's first wife and mother of his three children, Féla (née Felicie Poznanska), was Jewish.

this cold reasoner to prophesy! . . . Or was it just simply through atavism that this clairvoyant man, swept
away by a kind of verbal delirium, blinded himself to
the point of wishing to apply to the future the figures
of a very recent past, as if the future were nothing but
the product of divisions and multiplications, spring-
ing forth from his verified calculations! . . . I wasn't
listening anymore. It borders on fraud, for too many
people give themselves up today to this brand of
pythonism.

Loeb had seriously begun to bore me, and I was
finding the crossing of the American continent inter-
minable, when all of a sudden I burst out laughing.

Where was I?

No . . . it's not possible! . . . Was I really on the
train, in America, in the twentieth century? . . . and not
in the middle of the eighteenth century, on a Russian
telegue among the retinue traversing the Ukrainian
steppes during the memorable voyage of Catherine II
in Crimea . . . as I had just had the sudden illumination?

Why, these adobe train stations of the cook, the
manager Fred Harvey are the equivalent of the famous

movable scenes that Prince Potemkin erected on the horizon along the entire route through his domain in order to delude himself about the level of civilization and prosperity of his immense empire!

What a great joke! But who did they want to deceive here, in this democracy, if not the sovereign populace, in other words, the American citizen, the proudest man on earth and who gladly takes himself for the exemplary fellow, the paragon, the phoenix of the twentieth century!

"Loeb, my dear," I said to him, "like all of your compatriots, you are a victim of set design. Here, take a look . . . "

The train pulled out of Lamy. The train station, the station-hotel *El Ortiz* with its Indian porch and its Mexican courtyard, resembled one of those inns in Montmartre with a decorative stucco entry leading to a stylized garden. We might have thought ourselves on the Place du Tertre[15] or *Au Billard en Bois*, chez Fanny. And to complete the illusion, a hick dressed up

---

15. One of the most picturesque squares in Montmartre.

as a cowboy and holding a stack of handbills waited for confused customers on the platform of this huge adobe station, where no one stepped off the train.

The last cowboy in a pasteboard set planted in the New Mexican desert!

I will always remember the vision of that poor devil, standing in worn-out boots, squinting as he watched the deluxe train take leave, chewing tobacco and salivating in the sunlight.

"Did you see that man?" I asked my friend. "Have you made a place for him in your plan? Loeb, I think your numbers have deceived you. Prince Ligne[16] has already recounted in his *Memoirs* that the engineers brought in from foreign countries by Semiramis of the North to equip Russia had calculated that . . ."

But Loeb, furious, gathered up his papers and left the dining car to go lie down in his cabin. . . .

---

16. Charles Joseph Ligne, 1735–1814. Austrian field marshal, celebrated raconteur, and author of numerous letters and memoirs.

It wasn't the first time I had discovered that statisticians aren't too fond of mankind and loathe history. They're generally vain. To doubt their figures is to insult their true love, for they are sensitive. . . . Loeb and I were to have met up in California; I had given him my address, at the Garden of Allah in Hollywood. He was supposed to have phoned me, but he never did. We haven't seen each other again. But I learned from the local newspapers that he went on with his round of conferences.

With a great deal of success, yes, a great deal of success.

Ah, these lecturers, what a plague!

They are the traveling salesmen of culture. They pack their phoney wares, pose problems, offer solutions, distribute recipes, practice a little *dumping*.

They lie about everything, and believe it.

III

Mecca of the
Movies

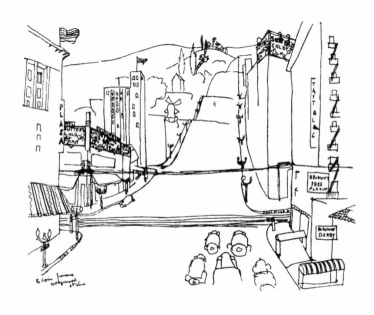

The Famous Corner of
Hollywood & Vine

IF YOU WANT TO MAKE MOVIES,

COME TO HOLLYWOOD; BUT UNLESS YOU PAY

THE PRICE, YOU WON'T SUCCEED!

When you get off the train in Los Angeles, you're practically thrown into the street!

Los Angeles has many beautiful skyscrapers, but the big city's train station is plainly insufficient. The long transcontinental trains slow to a stop and shove off again in the street. Thus, from the second you step out of your coach, you enter at ground level into the jumbled racket of trams, buses, and taxis.

Grab whichever one of these passing vehicles, toss the driver an address, race off, or head out on foot; from that moment on I defy you not to feel lost in the streets, above all if, like so many others, you've made your way to Hollwood with the hope of some day making movies.

In Hollywood, all roads lead . . . to a studio! So, at whatever pace you want to walk and no matter which direction you choose or how much time you take to get your bearings, any one of these streets intersecting in front of you and taking off in straight lines to the East, to the West, to the South, to the North, ends fatally at a wall.

This wall is the famous Great Wall of China that surrounds every studio and that makes Hollywood, already a difficult city to conquer, a true forbidden city — actually, either better or worse than that, since Hollywood is comprised of many interior barriers encircling numerous kremlins and defending access to dozens of seraglios, and I believe it is not only because of the radiance of the stars and the attraction they exert the world over that we have baptized Hollywood (where the advertising *slogan* is: *Hollywood, where the stars shine day and night*) Mecca of the Movies, but, strictly speaking, above all because the entrances to these studios are nearly impassable for the noninitiate, as if, really, to wish to make your way into a studio is to want to force entry into the Holy of Holies.

So, if you want to make movies in Hollywood, come on! . . . but announce it with a maximum of publicity, create a sensation, otherwise, unless you're willing to pay the price, you'll never get through, for there is the wall.

THE BREAK IN THE WALL

This wall, which surrounds every studio, is pierced by one small opening where, without fail, there is a crowd, since all other outlets in the enclosure are barricaded, grilled over, bolted, closed.

This tiny opening, this narrow, half-open door leads into a corridor or antechamber where you will find the blessed studio entrance through which so many long to slip.

But before being allowed to step across the threshold and push, heart pounding, through the turnstile that lets you in and chimes wickedly behind your back upon registering your entry, you are required, no matter who you are, to stand in a long line at a window open in the back wall, into which is embedded the anonymous head of a Pharisee, a head that belongs to the Cerberus of the place.

Head? What am I saying! This gatekeeper, now barking, now whispering into the telephone, no matter how many copies of him have been turned out, no matter what his type — brutal, a killjoy, sad, impassive, breezy, crafty, ill-tempered, cold, exaggeratedly polite, bewildered, a dimwit, narrow-minded, mean, dreamy or smiling — this monster of hypocrisy always made me think, every time, of what I would like to have done to him (which is why I had to watch myself), to this guardian of pagan hell, who, as everyone knows, was a dog with three heads: the first always raised to the sky, howling at the moon, the second, with glowering eyes, slavering, foaming at the mouth, and snarling ceaselessly, the third, whom no one trusts because she's always cringing and pretending to be asleep, given to sudden lunges so as to bite from behind the ankles of the damned as they pass by. . . . And, actually, it was the damned that these passersby standing around at the studio gates made me think about, waiting patiently without ever losing heart for a message from inside or the goodwill of a lying gatekeeper who

Entrance to the Studios (Universal) —
Helen Westey

just wants to be rid of them, all of these common folk of humble means, but enthusiasts of the cinema keeping the faith; men, women, boys, girls, little children flocked from every city in the world to wait in attendance at the gates to the underworld of this artificial paradise of the movies!

THE PHARISEES

Dante placed above the gate that descends into the regions of hell the famous inscription: *"Abandon all hope, ye who enter here . . ."*

In Hollywood they're a lot more brief, a lot more direct, a lot more cynical. They're not hampered by having to come up with a beautiful phrase. They tell people exactly what they feel the need to tell them, and not being able to tell them brutally enough in four letters, they let them know it in three words. They post above the door, for the benefit of those who insist on wanting to come in, a placard: *Do not enter.* That's it, period. So much the worse for those who don't understand, so much the worse for those who end up cracking their noses or breaking bones, and so much the worse, or so much the better, for those who finally succeed in getting through. We'll see soon enough what will happen to them then!

AT UNIVERSAL

So it is that at the entrance to Universal Films, beneath the window occupied by a dummy representative of Cerberus, whose head my friend Jean Guérin knew how to draw so well (it's a fairly prevalent type among the common herd in America), a sign is nailed up that reads: *It's useless to wait. — It's useless to insist. — You're wasting your time. — Recommendations won't get you anywhere. — This place was not meant for you. — Do not enter.*

With that, you've been warned.

But as Carl Laemmle, the president of this company, had in any case launched a frenzied publicity campaign in the newspapers, printing notices signed in his name in which he personally asks the public to please be so kind as to collaborate with him by sending in observations, comments, suggestions, promising to pay from \$50 to \$100 in *cash* if one of the submitted ideas was accepted, it was perhaps at the gate of Universal that the most suckers were cooling their heels.

These poor folks may not have understood anything of the gatekeeper's ostracizing them, but I'll swear between us that this sort of shriveled chameleon playing dumb always feigned not to know who we were talking about when we gave him one of the names of the company's bosses, and even when we handed him an urgent, signed notice, he played the innocent and claimed not to know where it came from!

AT PARAMOUNT

At Paramount, the whole team that works the window is of the boxing kind. They're young, beefy fellows, quick on their feet, and very determined. And they're not in "sports" for nothing! If your name is Durand, they announce Mr. Dupont, and if you ask to be put in contact with a Mr. Adam, they coolly address you to a Mr. Cook.

One day, one of these young swashbucklers who had made me spell three times not "Constantinople," but my name, and who had noted it correctly right in front of me, *C-e-n-∂-r-a-r-∂*, had the effrontery to announce to a starlet who was waiting for me, thinking I wouldn't catch the name he was conjuring on the telephone, *"that a certain Mr. Wilson wanted to see her"*!

You have to believe that such con games are in wide use at this firm, and that this chamber of lunatic concierges had the run of the place, because every time a Paramount department head makes an appointment with you he's obliged to come down himself or to send his secretary to fill out an entrance pass in advance, a simple phone call from him not being enough to cut through the temperamental moods of the boxers. Anyway, this piece of paper is often found having gone astray by the time you present yourself at the window at the appropriate hour, which is exactly what happened to me on another day when Charles Boyer, who could spare but one short hour for lunch, died of both boredom and hunger while waiting for me in the studio commissary, as a young preoccupied athlete who had misplaced my entrance permit suggested I apply myself to the instructions he had from Cerberus, who

The Window (Universal)

wasn't about to permit anyone to enter! I had to parley
for three-quarters of an hour and unsettle twenty people before winning my case, which was just to get in . . .
and go about finding Charles Boyer, who ended up
taking off without eating, since he had run out of time.

AT UNITED ARTISTS

At United Artists, the window clerk is not only a completely different type from the young boxers in train-
ing at Paramount, he is also from another generation
and even of an entirely different social extraction, as
befits this right-minded firm, the most distinguished in
the world of cinema and the only one in Hollywood to
dabble in refinement and civility.

It is, accordingly, a gracious man who assists me
when I show up, a distinguished gentleman with
grand, patronizing gestures, and this dear man is in
such a hurry to accommodate me that he can't even
wait for me to form a thought or pronounce a name
before he has already pushed a button and the door
opens in front of me. As I begin to move forward, this
gentleman-Cerberus rises and accompanies me three

steps, the better to clarify the directions he gives me. I am overwhelmed, beside myself with thank yous.

There's no doubt about it, I follow his instructions to the letter: South Courtyard, Building 39, Corridor B, Stairway III, 1st Floor, Office 13 . . . and when I arrive at my destination, I enter an office, heated of course, with a red rose in a vase, cigarettes, matches, a ream of white paper, exquisitely sharpened pencils, the day's newspapers, an office without one particle of dust, but an office in which there is absolutely no one and in which the telephone is deaf-mute!

I went back three times to this imperturbable straight-faced joker from United Artists, and each time he spun me onto the same outrageous course. Now that I think of it, this didn't really surprise me that much because at first sight I had thought there was something fishy about this gentleman, with his head like some old saint in an almanac which ought to have been bearded and covered with hair but which had in fact just been sheared with an electric razor and then polished, something that was stupefying, comic, inconceivable, even for an alien, but it Americanized him in a way that was somehow extremely suspect.

The third time, realizing that all of this blasted wag's directions were false, I thought it was hilarious and took advantage of the situation by going on an adventure through these vast studios that house a dozen or so enterprises, among them Mary Pickford's company.

The offices pertaining to this latter, into which I glanced indiscreetly in passing, were composed of a series of daintily furnished rooms draped in Liberty print cloth, with spinsters leaning over their typewriters as if over sewing machines (Mary Pickford is now Hollywood's lady patroness) and a darling little white doggie, no bigger than a ball of wool, splashed onto the carpet like a cream puff from a tea table.

It was also on that day that I encountered, coming around the corner of a building and slipping furtively into a courtyard, Douglas Fairbanks, whom the newspapers had announced was still in Cannes and whom I surprised returning incognito to this establishment, which was his at one time and perhaps still is, half of it anyway. The two of us, buttoned into our raincoats, collars up, hats cocked over our eyes on account of the rain, we had the air of a couple of thieves. Having passed by quickly without really noticing me, he turned around to see who I was, but didn't recognize me . . . and as for me, I didn't run after him to shake his hand, figuring that Doug didn't want to have been sighted. . . .

AT M.G.M.

At Metro-Goldwyn-Mayer, the first time I went there, hundreds of Japanese sailors were blocking the corridor. Clearing a path for myself among them, I thought I was plowing through a bunch of uniformed extras. But I was wrong, that's how you'll get fooled every step of the way in the free-for-all of the Hollywood studios, because you never really know if the person whose feet you have just stepped on is a real or a phoney character, least of all when that person is wearing a uniform or is decorated.

But sure enough, my Japanese mariners were the real thing, bona fide sailors. They were on shore

Restaurant (Universal) — Lunch with
Cendrars: Ed Arnold, Pinki Tomkin,
Helen Westey, etc.

leave from a battle cruiser of the Imperial Navy and had come to make a tour of Hollywood, and they all wanted to see — I heard this with my own ears when it was almost my turn to approach the window — *"the Missus Roma and the Mista Djuliet!"* M.G.M. having been filming just then Shakespeare's *Romeo and Juliet*, with the blazing Norma Shearer in the starring role.

Now, everyone knows that this star is a capricious creature who can't stand the presence of the least stranger on the set when she's filming because it makes her nervous and drains her of all her powers.

Which is to say that the Japanese were getting very upset and that the Cerberus at hand ought to have had a hundred reasons to be frazzled that morning. Absolutely not! This extraordinarily cool and prodigiously dextrous man, a veritable Cerberus-virtuoso, astounded me, for he certainly had a lot more guts than Napoléon, and the number of people he was in the midst of executing when it came my turn to meet him flooded me with admiration.

It's said that Napoléon dictated his mail to ten secretaries at once; the gatekeeper at M.G.M., he

spoke into and answered eleven telephones at once.
He had a thicket of receivers in each hand, Japanese
harassing him in gibberish, and if he was patched in
to Norma Shearer or to someone on her general staff,
they were saying god only knows what on the other
end, and surely things that were none too pleasant
for him — none of which kept him from asking me
(he had a very strong German accent) what it was I
wanted and, what rapture! from putting me immediately in touch with Mr. Vogel, Mr. Robert M. W.
Vogel himself, chief of international publicity and the
man I actually wanted to see, and not some Mr. Levy,
a name they spell *Lavee* over there, not for camouflage
but in accordance with local pronunciation.

As it was the only time I was received right
away in Hollywood, I have often asked myself since
whether or not it was due to an error or to some
happy coincidence, or if, in this powerful German-
American trust,[17] good practical sense and German

---

17. Since M.G.M. does not seem to have been owned even in part by
a German concern, one can only presume that this was yet another
tongue-in-cheek embellishment.

order weren't in the process — since a solid native accent cuts through the fluent English of most of this company's employees — of exerting pressure, of reducing the complications, the nonsense, the red tape of a meddlesome and bureaucratic administration, and of setting a famous example of efficiency and energy for the American organization, so often frivolous, wanton, or full of gaps, or else which runs in neutral, is an inhuman luxury, pure technicality, an art for art's sake.

And if I tell you that I asked around and discovered that this Cerberus-virtuoso was a young Nazi fresh off the boat from Germany, would we be able to draw certain conclusions?

Maybe so . . .

IV

New Byzantium

At the Trocadero
(encounter with Marlene Dietrich
and Greta Garbo)

FROM MATHEMATICS TO MYTH

Three rail lines connect the American east to the *Far West*. These rail lines are in fierce competition for comfort and speed. Three super-express transcontinental airlines, among them TWA, the famous Lindbergh line, vie for comfort and affordability with the railroads. Three modern highways stretch in a straight line *from coast to coast*, from the Atlantic to the Pacific, and along these straight lines rush innumerable brightly colored and aerodynamic buses that roll day and night (at dusk the conductor pulls a lever, all of the armchairs tip at once, and the tourists find themselves stretched out in a lying position!). They take ten full days to travel between New York, San Francisco and Los Angeles, and everyone rides them because of their unbelievably cheap fare — $30 —

while the train, which takes three and a half days, costs $130, and the plane, which gets you there in only eighteen hours, $160. Dozens upon dozens of ships, flying the colors of every country, directly link the ports of Europe and Asia with those of California. Without even mentioning the auto routes, railroads, airlines, and shipping lanes that come up from Mexico and down from Canada, the traffic converging from all cardinal points upon Hollywood is such that you've almost always got to reserve your places in advance.

It isn't surprising, you say, to see that all of this is happening in America, that Americans can't sit still and that the devotees of cinema don't count for much in the midst of a whole planet attracted by Hollywood for reasons of love, money, fame, power and prestige, making a name, exchanging ideas, the future, creation, art.

But you're forgetting that as America is the land of the fourth dimension, whatever goes on there immediately takes on such proportions that everything becomes vertiginous, and life itself — through the multiplication of a million bits of news and small but very precise details, cut into facets, each reflecting the other into infinity and deluding out of sheer repetition — in no time at all seems to have become unreal, a myth.

750,000 PHOTOGRAPHS,
35,000 LOVE LETTERS

Who would have thought that in 1935 Paramount alone would have sent out 750,000 photographs of its players addressed to the press and to *fans*, in other words, fanatics of film who wrote in and asked for them, and that Clara Bow, who has broken all known records in *sex appeal*, is known to have received as many as 35,000 love letters in a single week!

Given that there are at least eight great cinematic trusts in Hollywood and I don't know how many dozens, even hundreds, of stars, we can well imagine the postal volume that this international mail represents on a daily basis, and the movement of curiosity, and thus of attraction, witnessed by way of this immense correspondence.

A FACTORY OR A TEMPLE?

The human tide of interest and enthusiasm unleashed by the movies has become so threatening to Hollywood that Hollywood has had to take inhuman and lopsided defensive measures to hold back this frenzy fed by its own publicity, which is why everything in this vicious circle is such a total put-on.

For the wall surrounding every studio isn't only a symbolic wall, as one might have believed, a wall separating life from dream, the land of the real from the world of imagination, it is also an honest-to-goodness rock wall on both sides of which a double tragedy plays itself out, typically American in the way the drama suddenly shatters into a cascade of episodes more often than not extremely comic. (If you've already been bowled over by the spitefulness and ferocity frequently radiating from American comedies, you won't have any problem understanding that these films, even the most goofball and fast-paced, take their inspiration directly from reality and from life, and that their development, their *tempo*, are the result of keen observation, and therefore true.)

Outside of this enclosure, human waves roll in to kick their feet against the wall and beach themselves at the studio doors; inside, illustrious beings, famous, certainly, but of flesh and blood, captives of the studios, slaves, many of whom dream of nothing but escape, ask for nothing but to be allowed to leave, to live.

Except for maybe Monte Carlo, there isn't a city on earth where we kill ourselves more often than in Hollywood in the milieu of the movies — and it is also in this sense that despite its solidity the enclosure is nevertheless a symbolic wall: The opening that pierces it is utterly without parallel, since the studios into which it leads are the factories of illusion, and this world-renowned factory is for many a temple.

"TAEDIUM VITAE"

City Hall, the Hotel de Ville of Los Angeles, mother-city of Hollywood, is a tall, proud, and cold monument. When you're standing in front of it, it has such lovely balance, it seems so firmly planted on the ground and looks like such a pure product of reason, equilibrium, and plumb lines that one hesitates to enter into it to consult the index cards of unreason and despair.

Nevertheless, it is in this building, on the seventeenth floor, in a small office, the office of the census bureau, that we are able to learn, documents in hand, the annual number of the disillusioned of both sexes who take or try to take their own lives under the beautiful California sun.

These documents are kept scrupulously up-to-date, and the index cards filed first according to year, then according to the age of the despairing, and finally by category: those who committed suicide because they were compromised in a drug-related or moral affair, because they were in prison or avoiding arrest, because of domestic, financial, or love affairs, so as to avoid going to school [*sic*] or because they were reprimanded by their parents, crazy, drunk, high, disgusted with life in general, after having lost a loved one, for reasons of health, or young pregnant girls, et cetera, et cetera . . .

From this heap of official documents I copied for you only the following two sets of statistics:

Year: 1930

City	Population	No. of suicides	% per 100,000	Rate %	Progression
New York	6,930,445	1,378	19	204	+
Chicago	3,376,438	540	16	172	+
Philadelphia	1,950,961	332	10	107	+
Detroit	1,568,662	208	13	139	+
Los Angeles	1,238,048	439	35	374	+

Year: June 1932 — July 1933 (Los Angeles)

Method	Suicides			Attempts		
	Males	*Females*	*Total*	*Males*	*Females*	*Total*
Fire	0	1	1	0	0	0
Water	5	1	6	1	1	2
Gas	32	22	54	56	57	113
Firearms	152	21	173	12	7	19
Hanging	31	10	41	1	1	2
Chloroform	6	1	7	1	3	4
By throwing themselves in front of a moving vehicle	3	0	3	0	0	0
By throwing themselves from a bridge or skyscraper	13	12	25	2	7	9
By jumping from a moving vehicle	0	1	1	0	0	0
Knife, Scissors, Broken glass	7	0	7	16	5	21
Razor	6	2	8	34	21	55
Poison	61	54	115	128	438	566
Unknown	2	0	2	0	1	1
Totals	318	125	443	251	541	792

% 　　443 *suicides:*　　*Males* 72%　　*Females* 28%
　　　792 *attempts:*　　*Males* 32%　　*Females* 68%

The first set of statistics shows that of the five largest cities in the United States, Los Angeles places first proportionally with 439 suicides in 1930, and the second set gives a breakdown of the method of death chosen or attempted by 1,235 of the hopeless of both sexes in 1933 (out of decency they didn't want me to make copies of more recent statistics because of the names mentioned there). I will point out, moreover, that throughout America suicides are on the rise.

THE SHADOW OF THE STARS

Now then, if we ask the authorities in Los Angeles to what they attribute this sad record, the head of the census bureau at City Hall will put the high rate of suicide down to the California sun, "which easily disturbs the activities of the brain," as he contended, glaringly contradicting his colleagues: the head of the department of public health, who recorded 332 days of perfect sunshine in 1935 — "something that isn't a curse upon anyone, least of all the poor," he said, "for where the sun goes, medicine does not enter" — and the director of the office of publicity for tourism and recreation, which posts everywhere the slogan "Come to California — *sun-kissed Califor-nia*," a phrase that might be the beginning of a Vedic hymn. I am reminded, as a matter of fact, that these two high-ranking officials from the city of Los Angeles are, in their optimistic declarations, in agreement with the testimony of the ancient Spanish chroniclers of the sixteenth and seventeenth centuries who long ago also extolled the ideal California climate and the superiority of its sunshine; therefore, Frederick L. Hoffman, head of the census bureau, this small grumpy, red-haired man with thick glasses, must be wrong.

. . . But isn't it rather a matter of that artificial sun tapped by the Hollywood studios, which flares up every night in movie theaters around the world, and whose animated beam, loud, luminous, but charged with a strange light, indeed troubles the brain, causing the tragic shadow of the Star to sweep invisibly over Hollywood in broad daylight, and eclipse or shock on return, to strike at the heart of the disillusioned and the stars? . . .

ATMOSPHERE OF THE FACTORY
AND THE HOTHOUSE

This altogether melancholic vision appears completely false when you take a walk down the cheerful, lively streets of Hollywood, where automobiles filled with carefree youngsters besiege drive-ins serving sandwiches, hamburgers, and beer (are they really in so much of a hurry or are they just simply lazy, all these young men and women chasing fantasy who won't get out of their cars even when they eat?); but it seems much more plausible when you enter the superheated studios, whose factory and hothouse atmosphere is as oppressive as it is bizarre.

Having made and directed movies myself for many years in the days of the "silents," upon stepping into a Hollywood studio for the first time I was certainly a lot less surprised or entertained than someone else might have been, a kindly visitor or a noninitiate, for example, by the picturesque, the unexpected, the goings-on around a film shoot; however, I immediately noticed the difference "sound" has brought to the work now taking place on the set.

I'm not referring to the improvements, nor to the transformations in studio equipment, and even less to the colossal, complex, refined apparatus that the new technique of sound has introduced or requires today, for I find that normal after a ten-year absence from the studios; but I want to say something about the work I see going on everywhere, and about the method of working of all of the collaborators on a film.

HIGHLY ORGANIZED BUT JOYLESS LABOR

What strikes me right away upon going in is to see the large numbers of people crowding the sets these days and busying themselves around the director and his cast.

Since not one minute can be lost, as there are no work stoppages, not a moment's hesitation in the pace of the work, in short, since it "runs smoothly" from dawn to dusk, with the merest break at lunchtime, I have concluded that, as in a factory, everyone knows exactly what he has to do, and it didn't take me long to figure out that the crew surrounding the director is today composed entirely of specialists. But just as quickly I also had the feeling that this continuous,

hurried work lacked spirit, and that if every man bus-
tling about in his corner really knows his place, does
his job quasi-automatically, he takes no interest in the
overall effort, doesn't give a moment's thought to the
end result, which is for all that a work of art.

Apart from the title and the director, and perhaps
also the principal actors in the film, I strongly doubt
that the crew knows more than what it's doing, so
great was the haste I saw to get the day's tasks over
with, which are done swiftly, for sure, but without joy.

So many feet, so many scenes an hour on such and
such a set. Each day the task is assigned. And they bow
before it. And everyone is extremely tense. From time
to time someone lights up a cigarette to relax. But from
the director and the star to the last electrician and the
lowliest prop man, no one seems content, since everyone feels watched by the timekeepers and experts who
have divided the screenplay into minutes, set up the
work schedule, handed out roles, determined functions,
posts, calculated expenses, responsibilities, the stakes as
well as the scale of salaries. True enough, the salaries
are up there, way up there, but then, so are the stakes ...

Nevertheless, under these conditions, this studio work — which no longer has anything artistic about it but is repetitive, exhausting, backbreaking for everyone — ultimately frustrates, displeases, and discourages artists with personality and talent who see all of their gifts imprisoned in the same job year in and year out, as the living beauty of the stars, which everyone strives to fix once and for all into a type that must remain forever unchanged, rapidly fades or goes out of fashion, or as the most gifted director, the richest in ideas, is crushed.

It's just that discipline is very strict on the Hollywood sets, and the rule is inflexible: They don't ask you to be a genius, but to obey and do it fast.

RATIONALIZATION

So it is that owing to the force of circumstances and for having wanted too much to rationalize an art that has given birth to one of the foremost industries in the modern world (the American movie moguls, who invest hundreds of millions of dollars every year in the entertainment industry, grossed $2.3 billion at the box

offices in 1929, the year of the great Crash; and Harold
Loeb claimed on the train that with his "plenty" they
would have grossed 5 billion!), the technicians of
sound are left with a repetitive, assembly-line business
perhaps more economical, and even more lucrative for
the producers and the trusts, but disappointing for all
of the other collaborators on the film, since this ratio-
nalization has transformed the unfettered work of
artistic creation, in the Hollywood studios, into a series
of recipes and scheduled, though bizarre, operations,
complicated to the point that the art of a shoot is today
less an art than a Byzantine ritual.

That's why you've got to have at least fifty people around to capture the close-up of a kiss, and why
one film idea has to pass through the sixty-eight specialized departments that make up a huge movie company before it's finished and finally projected onto the
screen in a public theater!

THE PARADE OF THE KISS

Here's the rundown of the fifty people whose presence is indispensable for capturing the close-up of a

Irene Dunne Filming *Show Boat*

kiss exchanged by a young amorous couple, placed
for example in a clearing and thinking themselves . . .
alone at last!

"Kiss me now, darling," says the young man, and
the young woman offers him her lips, chastely, lan-
guorously, passionately, greedily, surprised, fright-
ened, with hesitation or with fire and ecstasy, et cetera,
et cetera, et cetera . . .

To record this scene — banal and minor but
important since it's probably just to see it that millions upon millions of other couples will stay up late
every night at the movies, and why Will Hays, the
dictator, the American Czar of worldwide cinematic
censorship, this Quai d'Orsay with three hundred
embassies, has personally interfered on many occa-
sions with the great firms in order to regulate and
time the duration of a kiss — it therefore requires
the presence of: first, the two artists. Then there has
to be: one director, two assistants to the director,
two *script girls* (secretaries to the director); two cameramen, two assistant cameramen, two assistants to
the cameramen (to carry the camera), a still photog-

rapher; three stagehands, two prop men, a painter; four electricians, a chief electrician, three generator mechanics; a sound engineer, called a mixer, a microphone operator, an assistant microphone operator (to carry the device), a sound recorder (isolated in his booth); two doubles for the actors; a valet, a maid, a professional male or female dresser, a master makeup artist; two supply stewards to carry and serve lunch for everyone; a driver for the catering truck, seven chauffeurs for the cast's rental cars, a driver for the generator truck, a driver for the prop truck, a driver for the electricians' truck, a driver for the sound truck.

Add it all together, we come up with fifty.

You think there's no one else around our amorous couple and now you're really going to say I'm exaggerating if I add someone else? . . . But yes, there is someone else, someone who frets constantly and thinks everyone's just taking it easy, that the whole thing's dragging, that it's never right, that this kiss . . .

"Look, kids, let's go, let's go, get it right for once, move it! . . ."

It's the producer munching on his cigar with rage while thinking about the insane amount of money this kiss is costing and about the immense sum it can bring in . . . and if the producer isn't there in person, it's his brother or his nephew, maybe even his entire family, his wife, his wife's girlfriends . . .

So, there are a lot more than fifty, and every one of them chatters, quibbles, gossips, compares, hands out advice, comments, bursts out laughing, smiles, envies, censors, applauds this kiss — this fake kiss — and when it's all over, the whole petticoated, cackling tribe goes out on the town for a cocktail, a *Kiss-me-quick*, Mae West's favorite, at the Vendome or the Trocadero, the two most fashionable night spots.

THE METAMORPHOSIS OF THE IDEA

If you have an idea for a script, don't put it down in writing and, as tempting as mailboxes can be, don't mail it to Hollywood, and above all don't give yourself any illusions, because even if your idea is brilliant, it's not worth the postage: *It will be sent back to you without having been read.*

This process is an absolute law and the main raison d'être of the IDEA department, the first of the sixty-eight specialized departments that make up the organization of a large movie company through which a film must pass from conception to realization and exhibition.

Here's a list of the principal departments. I've written them down in the order of the function each performs in its turn for the successful completion of a film and to facilitate the general operation of so complicated an enterprise. It's hard to say what is more to be admired, the formality or the complexity of such an official organization. For my part, what astonishes me is that this Byzantine ensemble even works and that it turns out a film at all, good or bad.

Departments

I. IDEA. Not only does this department send back the scripts it finds in the mail *without reading them*, since it has its own, it also goes so far — with the goal of proving to the company's officials that it exercises a kind of monopoly on information and that outside of its domain there's no salvation — as to call for the ideas of others, as a ruse, much as a magistrate might make a false allegation in order to get at the truth. So the IDEA department organizes screenplay competitions with the ulterior motive of never putting into production the prizewinning work!

That's what happened during a recent competition, announced sensationally in the press by one of the big Hollywood studios, when eight IDEA specialists, who were each paid an additional $1,000 per week for their efforts, had to open, classify, and read the 30,000 scripts that came in, and not a single one of them was kept! But the title of the film announced for this competition, *The Ten Commandments*, was hurled at the general public with the maximum fanfare — and the sly announcers in the IDEA department were the ones who came up with it, along with this unprecedented promotional gimmick.

When the film came out, it gave rise to a host of plagiarism suits.

II. READING. This department feeds IDEA by providing it with suggestions. Everything published in the entire world is read there. Each firm reads about 25,000 volumes per year. These books are not only gone through and analyzed into a report, but reduced to the outline of a script, what is called in the sweet jargon of the industry a *synopsis*.

It is this synopsis, and not the book, or, as they say, the *original*, that is classified, catalogued, and sent into the archives, and it is this first anonymous outline, on the synopsis and not the book, that the studio's staff writers are called to work into a screenplay afterwards, if IDEA has accepted the concept of the book. That's why so many authors — Carco,[18] O'Flaherty,[19] myself, et cetera — no longer recognize their works once they've been brought to the screen.

In Hollywood, the author is considered an ass----. They've paid him for the rights, all he has to do is keep quiet.

III. EXECUTIVE. This department relays the idea from the IDEA service to the vendors and distributors scattered across the United States. It takes into

18. Francis Carco, 1886–1958. French poet and novelist.
19. Presumably Irish novelist Liam O'Flaherty, 1896–1984.

account the response of the agents who are in commercial contact with the exhibitors, who are themselves in daily contact with the theatergoing public. The EXECUTIVE department uses IDEA to modify the idea at hand according to the criticisms, advice, and opinions forwarded to it.

This department also keeps in contact with its foreign agents and even immediately begins to generate publicity around the idea for the film in order to watch the reaction overseas and, if necessary, to be able to make emergency corrections to the script.

This is the origin of so many false reports published in the international press every time Hollywood starts working on a new film.

IV. LEGAL. The LEGAL department takes on all questions of rights concerning the studio: contracts with authors and artists, copyrights, insurance, et cetera, et cetera. It has to consider a production from every legal aspect in order to avoid litigation and claims for damages, above all the libel suits, always extremely numerous, initiated by stray individuals, groups, communities, even an entire nation.

Despite the good nose, the caution, and the devotion of its experts in things cinematic, this department is overflowing with lawsuits for plagiarism, in which it is mired from January 1 to December 31. For instance, after the presentation of *King of Kings*, Cecil B. de Mille and Paramount saw themselves accused of plagiarism by a crank, a certain Miss Valeska Suratt, who dragged them before the court. At the last proceeding, the judge declared, in handing down his decision: ". . . if we were to properly uphold the accusation of plagiarism, Miss Suratt would first have to establish that she truly was the author of the Bible . . ." Upon which this madwoman began howling that indeed she was!

There are serious cases, but nine times out of ten the studios have to deal if not with lunatics, at least with rascals and swindlers or blackmailers, because cinema is a mother lode and everyone wants a piece of the action.

V. CONCEPTION. This department chooses the histories, negotiates the screen adaptation rights of a novel or play (preferably something fashionable or a hit). It is also this department that appoints from among the writers under contract to the studio the authors that seem most qualified for adapting a particular work or fleshing out such and such a subject.

The writers attached to the studio are always the authors of the screenplay. That's why on the poster Max Reinhardt and a few obscure authors (among them a young literature professor brought in specially from Cambridge) signed *A Midsummer Night's Dream* in place of Shakespeare without making anybody laugh . . . in Hollywood!

VI. BUDGETING. Once the idea is accepted, the financial service of BUDGETING studies the script and divides it into as many financial slices as there are departments to handle it.

BUDGETING assigns each section a specific budget that cannot be overrun for any reason. If one of these budgets has been underestimated, the department responsible for the amount must trim, economize, shift for itself in any way it can, show inventiveness, initiative — in short, it must manage on its own without harming the production.

A film must be made with the amount of money specifically earmarked for it. For a current production this amount varies from $25,000 to $2,000,000. They don't tolerate a deviation of one penny, and the whole amount must be spent. BUDGETING never goes back on its figures.

VII. RESEARCH. Types of questions posed on an average day in the RESEARCH department: What does the sea look like in Saragossa [*sic*]?

How many fasces did they carry before Caesar?

What is the color and license plate number of the car of the Brazilian consul in Bombay?

The Place de l'Alma in Paris, is it planted with chestnut or plane trees?

What kind of comb do the Javanese use? Material? Shape? Number of teeth?

Are there still night sessions at Bow Street? How is the room lit? Do the magistrates wear their wigs at night?

When available, RESEARCH will forward the information by phone, and if not, it will request it by cable from the four corners of the earth.

On Hollywood Boulevard
(The wearers of dark glasses hope to
be taken for stars — incognito!)

VIII. PRODUCTION. Is in contact with and selects the stars, the artists, the extras. Conducts screen tests.

IX. MAKEUP. Paints upon the faces of the actors the characteristics of the role they are going to play.

X. ART. Designs the plans and builds the models for the sets.

XI. CONSTRUCTION. This department consists of workshops for sawing, carpentry, joining, plastering, plumbing, painting, wallpapering, forging, zincworking, metalworking, glassworking, masonry, bricklaying, tilemaking, draperies, tapestries, gardening, et cetera, et cetera.

XII. STAGE. Furnishes the sets, provides all of the customary props that *figure* in a home to create a realistic atmosphere: Flowers, vases, china, silverware, household utensils, et cetera, from the living room to the kitchen, the wine cellar, the cow shed, or the nursery.

XIII. PROPS. Provides and is responsible for all of the props that *play a role* in a scene. These range from the toothpick a man uses when he leaves his table to the floating guns that must bring down the city walls of Alexandria.

XIV. FABRICATION. Makes at the studio all props not found in stores.

XV. WARDROBE. This department must not only provide all of the clothing from this century, but also the finery and armor from all eras and all countries. It consists of a fashion workshop, designers, costumers, buyers, cutters, tailors, seamstresses, embroiderers, furriers, feather artists, florists, jewelers, launderers, dry cleaners, cobblers, et cetera, et cetera.

XVI. SPECIAL EFFECTS. Conceives the techniques for every sensational trick. Responsible for the collision of two trains or two cars, stages the cataclysms at the end of the world, controls the parting and the closing of the waters of the Red Sea. This department has annihilated the word *impossible*.

XVII. BACK PROJECTION. Department specializing in trick photography . . . an unlimited field.

XVIII. SECRETARIAL. Hundreds and hundreds and hundreds of charming young women typing and copying in every department — since every studio blackens even more paper than it uses film.

XIX. MANAGEMENT. This department is the purgatory of the director, who bickers routinely with it about the daily schedule, the dividing up of the workload, the installation of the sets, the availability of the stages, and ... expenses.

. . . .

XXX. ELECTRICAL. Takes care of all lighting and electrical power, and this is no small affair in a studio. In a single scene of *Cleopatra*, four hundred miscellaneous devices were used on the stage and two hundred electricians were not underused to survey, adjust, operate light boxes, arc lamps, *sunlights*, stage lights, spotlights, incandescents, floods, follow spots, *babies*, light guns, torches. A chief electrical engineer must know how to light an ensemble shot like an impressionist painter or as Rembrandt knew how to distribute light in his eaux-fortes.

XXXI. CAMERA. The cameramen must be as sensitive as artists and as built as athletes. Sensitive for the composition of groups and the choice of camera angle; built and with nerves of steel, for the crank must turn smoothly under any circumstances and no matter what the risks.

XXXII. PHOTO. The photographers print shots and make studio portraits to advertise the film and for the pleasure of photo hobbyists.

XXXIII. SOUND. The mixer in his soundproof booth must be on the watch every moment of the film in order to instantaneously adjust his dial from a sigh to a cannonburst.

XXXIV. RENTAL. Rents all necessary equipment.

XXXV. MUSIC. Composers and musicians. Popular songs, incidental music. Symphony orchestra, organ, and jazz. Sound effects engineers and radio. Metro-Goldwyn-Mayer has the most important music library in the United States (I even found Satie's works there).

XXXVI. LABORATORY. Developing and printing. Sixty prints are struck of each Hollywood film.

XXXVII. PROJECTION. Each day directors and their general staff can watch the previous day's work.

XXXVIII. EDITING. The editor and cutter are dramatists. They must have an innate sense of action, rhythm, pacing, and "tempo." Their contribution to the intrinsic value of a film is estimated at 20%.

XXXIX. TITLES.

. . . .

XLV. FIRE AND EXPLOSIVES. The lives of the film crew are often in their hands, which is why every studio has its pyrotechnists, firemen, et cetera.

XLVI. HOSPITAL, MEDICAL SERVICES.

XLVII. VENTILATION.

XLVIII. MENAGERIE. All animals from the mouse to the elephant, through tigers, lions, snakes, birds, monkeys, fish. On the ranch, horses, flocks of sheep, herds of cows, poultry yard.

XLIX. TRANSPORTATION. Must be practically ready to transport an army at the drop of a dime. Provides trucks for moving tons upon tons of materiel, catering vans to guarantee meals for the extras, portable barracks to house everyone while camping "on location." In principal, must overcome all obstacles and be stopped by nothing.

L. LOCATION. Keeps in its archives an extraordinary documentation regarding sites, landscapes, dwellings, et cetera. Must be able to locate within twenty-four hours any foreign site within a fifty-mile range of Hollywood and have it camouflaged in detail. Recently a company was shooting a film in color in the desert and realized that the natural colors were too bland and did not enhance the new process patented by the company at great cost, and didn't balk at asking LOCATION to send tank trucks to spread the white desert sand with tons and tons of the chosen hues, so as to obtain beautiful iridescent colors on the screen and to be able to boast in its advertising of the unequaled chromatic refinement of its filming process and the hypersensitivity of its direct color photography!

LI. COMMISSARY. Runs the restaurant. Must be able to serve two thousand lunches in record time, at the studio or in the desert.

LII. DIRECTOR. He's a general and a conductor. Must know how to command, but must also manage to coordinate through flexibility and diplomacy the efforts of all of the services collaborating in the production of his film. His biggest enemies are wasted time and loss of money. Must know how to inspire his actors, but above all the bureaucrats at the head of every department who tend to want to escape his supervision. Must be perpetually on the lookout and watch that no one strays from the strict and precise parameters of his direction under the pretense of specialization or for the sake of art. Must have the will and the tact to know how to get the script respected by all. Is the champion of the idea.

. . . .

We have now come full circle back to the idea for the screenplay. But the idea, though filmed, hasn't reached the end of its misadventures.

LX. The PRODUCTION department takes over.

LXI. DIALOGUE changes it.

LXII. DUBBING modifies it.

LXIII. CENSORSHIP dissects it, cuts it, circumcises it.

LXIV. FAN MAIL praises it to the skies.

LXV. PUBLICITY colors it, puffs it up, makes it explode.

LXVI. MARKETING negotiates it.

LXVII. DISTRIBUTION multiplies it, spreads it around, vulgarizes it.

Finally, LXVIII, EXHIBITION trades it for cash. Don't ask me what it has become by then. The public applauds. That's enough.

Who was the classical philosopher who held that ideas were meant to be thought and not lived? In Hollywood, an industry has been born that lives by them and keeps the whole world living by them — which is the best proof that this New Byzantium really is the capital of the modern world.

BEHIND THE SCENES

You can't stroll around the way I did for entire days behind the scenes at 20th Century Fox, Paramount, M.G.M., or Warner Brothers — passing from one department to the next, for example from the Accounting Department, which receives totals electronically, minute by minute, and is kept automatically up-to-date by ingenious, joyous machines that never deceive and never make mistakes and that marvelously replace eight hundred timorous bookkeepers, to the conservation warehouses, where in an impressive silence and an odor of naphthalene you can not only wander for miles among the dresses, hats, lingerie, stockings, gloves, bodices, girdles, shoes, the trinkets carried by the queens of the silver screen, but where you can see, touch, fondle a complete collection of mannequins in wax or stuffed with horsehair modeled in the nude on the starlets themselves, whose breasts, necks, abdomens, thighs, hips, and backs are riddled with pins with large colored glass heads and covered with inscriptions in ink, marks giving, along with supporting dates, the most indiscreet and intimate measurements on the slow, fading physiology of the stars — without leaving in the evening absolutely dumbfounded by what you've seen or discovered and without spending part of the night mulling over the explanations, numbers, statistics each department head has overwhelmed you with and without thinking also about all the carping you've heard and the confidences that have been passed on to you during your visit.

EVERYONE IS UNHAPPY

It's a curious thing: Everyone is unhappy in Hollywood, and the further up a man is in the hierarchy of the studios, the greater his responsibility, the more money he makes, the more he thinks of himself as a victim or envied by his colleagues, or misunderstood, or neglected, or kept on the sidelines by the big bosses. In short, every department head imagines he isn't where he is supposed to be and deserves a better position, or else he thinks that it's his whole department that isn't playing the role it ought to have in the production of a film, that they don't appreciate his contribution for its true worth, that his advice isn't taken enough into account, that no one listens to his suggestions, that some other department is infringing on his territory, that it's skimming from his budgets, that everyone wants to strangle him.

For these high-placed bureaucrats, each confined to his own department, criticizing, competing with each other, the arrival of a foreign journalist is quite a godsend, and they take advantage of it to relieve their bitterness, and that's no lie. To hear them tell it, the movie business is screwed.

V

Mystique or
Sex Appeal?

Sandwich Stand

THE GREAT ZIEGFELD

It was on a stage at M.G.M. They were filming *The Great Ziegfeld*, the already legendary life of the king of Broadway, of this man of theatrical extravaganzas who had astounded New York for a quarter of a century, of this impulsive, profligate businessman, this inspired bluffer of an adman, the Ziegfeld of twenty super-spectacular musical revues, every one of which was a milestone in theater, the Ziegfeld who launched stars upon stars in bouquets, most of whom left a lasting mark in the music hall, this director who deliberately gave in to overbidding, not to flatter "his" public, but to rouse it even more, all while imposing upon it his art and his taste as a brazen innovator and drawing them into his own orbit, this impresario whose every spectacle — always too sumptuous and,

it's true, often grandiloquent, but ever strangely, profoundly, humanely lyrical — was an attempt to crys-
tallize and convey to the stage popular longings for
beauty, the sparkle, the magnificence of dreams and
of riches; that's why the *Ziegfeld Girls* had to be the
prettiest girls in the world, just as the *Ziegfeld Follies*
had to be the most enchanting and costly spectacles
not only in America, but in the universe, something
this devil of a man, who spent more millions than he
earned, never allowed himself to stop pursuing and
undertaking, because despite his faults, his childish
vanity, his love of uproarious publicity and of immediate returns, his desire to astonish, his fast-talking,
the pettiness of a small tyrant redeemed by lavish
gestures, Monsieur Ziegfeld had an authentic conception of glory.

NEW YORK BY NIGHT

And it is this itch for glory, this insatiable appetite that
gives to his thrilling and adventurous life, full of ups
and downs, and to his baroque, dense, stunning work,
a unity that only cinema was able to express in carry-

ing this incomparable career to the screen, and that the film — the shooting of which I had the opportunity to witness — has actually rendered masterfully by creating the artistic unity of a grandiose spectacle whose authenticity doesn't so much rest in the biography of an individual as in the atmosphere, the evocation, the legend, the resurrection of an entire recent but defunct epoch, because only the cinema has been capable of telling as a simple biography the lived history of the tastes, fads, attractions, amusements, and distractions of the public, and the most frivolous, the most fickle, the most fleeting of all publics, that of the theaters of a great city and its pleasure havens: New York, Broadway by night, with its dancing, its dandies, its camouflaged prostitution, its worldly and street-level elegances, its fashions, feathers, jewelry, its nudes, its boys, its music, its flickering lights, its shimmering silk stockings, and a whole jumble of makeup — lashes, eyes, smiles, mouths, necks, painted or extended fingernails, shaven underarms, steaming backsides, voices coarsened by alcohol — and transparent lace underwear and crush-hats as a grand finale!

"LIGHTS! . . . ACTION! . . ."

The studio was jammed with jazz — pianos, violins, flutes, saxophones, the clangs of a gong, brass, drums. Thousands of clustered lamps sparkled, hundreds of spotlights heaved, capsized in the distance. Above the innumerable heads of the costumed actors and extras, the giant lever for panoramic shots moved about the battens in the loft, swinging Robert Z. Leonard, director of this admirable production honoring the cinema, his cameramen, and his team of helpers and electricians in tubs suspended in midair.

THE HAUNTING CHORUS FROM
THE NIGHTCLUB

All at once a man's voice rose and began to sing a sentimental nightclub refrain, a refrain then taken up by the orchestras and choirs, while onstage a complicated game of veils and glorious curtains glided on their rods, revealing little by little and by turns a gigantic monument, a kind of made-up mountain that swiveled slowly on its base, exposing progressively at each revolution fresh flocks of beautiful singing young girls, troupes of

Jeanette MacDonald Filming
San Francisco
(In the cooper's cap: Anita Loos)

male and female dancers, a whole motionless regiment of black outfits, standing perpendicularly with their backs around the enormous grooved barrel of the massive central column that rose and lost itself in the tropical, starry, night sky, and in every curl, on every landing of the spiral staircase that led toward the summit of this animated and vertiginous tower to a revolving platform lost high in the air, more and more young girls, tiered and as if drawn into the slow rotating movement of the constellations, took up, with smiles and nostalgia, the initial nightclub refrain that started it all and that now fell muted from above, just as the faraway music of the spheres reaches earth, softened, like a sweet murmur, from the breathtaking depths of the sky.

THE CLIMAX OF THE *ZIEGFELD FOLLIES*[20]

IS A PAGE TORN FROM MY NOVEL,

LE PLAN DE L'AIGUILLE

What was unfolding before my eyes, in a succession of dazzling tableaux, were so many scenes of love,

---

20. *Ziegfeld Follies* was the third film to use Florenz Ziegfeld's name, and was released in 1946. Cendrars refers again here to *The Great Ziegfeld*.

grace, joy, unconcern, and innocence developing into a poetry at once charming and unsettling since it was both anecdotal and cosmic, historical and unreal, and, despite its ineffable splendor, always of a profound, eternal, and genuine humanity.

So imagine my amazement when in the midst of my emotions I felt rising, bit by bit, the certainty of having already witnessed this spectacle as I recognized forming, reconstituting, materializing before my eyes, which could not believe this marvel because it was unfurling on another plane in an ambiance ringing with harmonies and all sparkling in the studio lights, page 89 of my novel, *Le Plan de L'Aiguille*, where I had described, ten years before, in the silence of the study, a similar monument of plastic synthesis and of life's apotheosis, which reads as follows:

> *A seething tangle of cyclopean beings formed the base*
> *of the monument. From this tangle escaped upright*
> *men, scrambling up the first tier of the mountain,*
> *clasping in their muscled arms women of all races.*
> *The women burst forth joyously from their grasp,*

laughing, light, startled. Like a swarm of butterflies or birds they fluttered in a spiral around the monument, whose height they nearly reached. But this summit was bulging. A cloud of round-faced children clung to it, boys and girls circling as they sang. In the midst of this circle sat an adolescent boy. He stood up. He moved around the summit as he gradually rose. Step by step, he climbed, now facing forward, now in profile, now away. Always higher. Always higher. Finally, he broke free alone into the void. He had reached the summit: a ball, a sphere, a globe, a lamp, the sun — which he tried to tear away, to raise and uphold, high, high up into the air, arms outstretched, without weakening. Prometheus! [21]

It's true that on the stage at M.G.M. my Prometheus was an adorable brunette, enthroned in clouds, with serious eyes, but luminous with happiness like the stars of the Southern Cross that show-

---

21. *Author's Note:* Blaise Cendrars, *Le Plan de l'Aiguille*, novel, 42d ed. (Paris, 1919), 89.

ered her as they crossed behind her head, and her smiling companions, who cartwheeled around her, were the radiant reflection of her unique beauty, multiplied from the center into infinity.

A SCRIPT GIRL IN ASSISI IN THE YEAR 1260:
ANGELA OF FOLIGNO[22]

But my emotion was so great upon seeing the birth and the live embodiment in Hollywood of what I had only dreamt and evoked in black on paper, one night, in my writer's room in Paris — and this formal and living materialization was of such a pure art — that rather than stop this spectacle, run to a lawyer to seize the film and claim a million dollars in damages from the film company, in the unexpected joy that this surprise gave me, and blessing the screenwriters for their fortunate plagiarism, I clung to the arm of the wonderful creature, a fine, intelligent, and supple Florentine, who allowed me to escort her to the

---

22. Saint Angela of Foligno, 1248–1309. Italian mystic born in Foligno, Umbria, author of *The Book of the Experiences of the Truly Faithful.*

Franz Lederer Filming
Monsieur Sans-Gêne

studio — where as a *script girl* she was one of the few
women of the elite in Hollywood — whose emotion I
also saw mounting and whose turmoil rose in a cre-
scendo in time with the progression of the spectacle,
growing in intensity and magnificence on the brink of
the finale; leaning toward her and whispering into
her ear, pointing at the young divine women, her sisters, whose multitude on the stage, whose apotheosis
made my head spin as their beauty ravished my soul,
I said:

"Watch, these are the Thrones, *bimba*. These
girls are no longer women, they are far too many and
too beautiful! Listen to this music. This nightclub
refrain has lost its vulgarity because of all it has successfully balanced and set in motion on the stage. I
don't know how you manage it, but here, in this studio, you're not making cinema anymore, it's high mys-
ticism. We are in the midst of heaven, and this
apotheosis, glorifying the beauty of women, whom we
admire, you and I, is no longer a worldly picture, it is
now a vision, a glance, a panoramic glimpse, like some
recording in the great beyond. You'll understand and

remember what your compatriot, the blessed and visionary Angela of Foligno, said when she spoke of the beauty of God and his escorting army of thundering angels: *"Their multitude was so dazzling and so perfectly innumerable that, IF NUMBER AND MEASURE WERE NOT LAWS OF CREATION, I would have believed I was watching a sublime throng without number and without measure. I could not see the end, either in width or in length, of this multitude, I saw throngs more vast than our highest figures . . ."*

"Oh, dear, I love you!" the young woman said to me with a mysterious smile while nudging me with her knee.

"You're an angel, *bimba*, just like all of the beauties here, exposed to the light. But, tell me, is it you, my Italian, who knew how to honor number and measure in this apotheosis whose grandeur crushes me? Tell me, did you know this mystic text?"

"Mystic, you say? In Hollywood we say *sex appeal*, it's more reliable . . ."

And the beautiful script girl began to hum the refrain that haunted us all, actors and assistants, the nightclub refrain, the miraculous refrain . . .

Then I kissed my patrician on the neck, scandalizing people in the studio.

Ah, these poets!

VI

The Great Mystery
of Sex Appeal

At Max Factor's

WALLY WESTMORE,
EXPERT ON SEX APPEAL

"No star without sex appeal, and no sex appeal without makeup. But without the perfect line for the hair, beauty is impossible . . ."

Such is the first aphorism of Wally Westmore, creator of the facial aesthetic of the movies.

Established for twenty years in Hollywood, where he has specialized in beauty care and made himself famous for his research and by his repeated and resounding successes, Wally Westmore, the master makeup artist at Paramount, is both the inventor and the manufacturer of most of the stars who have built worldwide reputations. And his judgment, like that of the Pope in religious matters, is considered infallible when it comes to beauty transported to the screen.

An expert on sex appeal, it is he who has subjected the most valued artists, and so the proudest and most untouchable, to the humiliation of a quarterly "physiological test" and who bestows upon each one of them her "personal chart of beauty," to which they all submit. In the same way, not one newcomer, not a single *starlet,* has a chance to succeed in the movies if Westmore, this clairvoyant magician, doesn't imprint her first with her "genre" and then with her "type."

Wally Westmore is the man who has done the most in the world to modernize, renovate, feminine charm by adding to its eternal mystery the attraction of the line of the hair, the line of the day, as a seduction.

THE KEY TO SEX APPEAL

"It is often said that the eyes are the windows of the soul, and that may be so after all — but the actual hairstyle of *Milady* is the key to her sex appeal," Westmore contends.

"The eyes, the mouth, the complexion, the figure might be impeccable and well-proportioned, but there's no real sex appeal for a woman without the architecture, the artifice of the hairstyle, because all of her natural charms will only be balanced by the line of her hair."

And he adds: "By this line I mean the symmetry, somehow aerial, or even, may I say, syncopated, that must link the lower and the upper part of the face before spreading and governing the rest of the face that includes the hard features, the soft or the blurred ones. A face poorly balanced by the placement and the mass of the hair could never seduce on the screen, since sex appeal is a radiance, a magnetic attraction, an emission or an exchange of waves, in a word: a harmony.

"Most of the stars' faults can be corrected through makeup, or lighting, or even photographic retouching; but if the mass and the placement of their hair is asymmetrical, or even if the line of their hairstyle is misplaced, all of our efforts will be in vain and their face will always appear disproportionate in its different parts, in other words it will seem counterfeit and tormented, thus, ugly.

"As Baudelaire said, 'I hate the movement that displaces . . . the line!' "

THE MOST BEAUTIFUL FACE OF THE DAY

The woman with the ideal hair line and the most perfect face, according to Wally Westmore, this connoisseur, passionate and sensitive to the point of comparing the divine face of this woman to a beating heart, is Gladys Swarthout, star of the Metropolitan Opera and of the recent movie *Give Us This Night*.

"Her forehead is neither too high nor too low," explains Westmore with emotion, "it curves slightly toward the center, giving her hair line a double curve in the shape of a heart, a noble design whose purity is reinforced — and with what grace! — by the fluttering narrowness of her temples."

Among the other stars whose hairstyles are in perfect harmony with their beauty type and who best illustrate Westmore's theory, since they all came to us through his creative hand, he prefers to name: Mae West, Jean Harlow, Kay Francis, Claudette Colbert, and Sylvia Sidney.

BLONDE NEGRESSES

We were standing beneath a billboard, Westmore and I, finding shelter from the pouring rain, but we were still being splashed. He was waiting for a kid who had gone to get his car in a *parking lot* flooded with a foot of water. Up to then, I hadn't breathed a word, I was too happy just to listen to the talk of this intriguing man whom I had been told was enigmatic and secretive. He allowed himself to confide in me and I pricked up my ears, troubled and surprised by a streak of melancholy in all of his thoughts. I felt he was worried, feverish, disdainful, even dissatisfied or disappointed. Perhaps his disgruntled mood was only caused by bad weather or overwork. As his car was still not ready, hoping to entertain him, I began telling him how I had found myself in Brazil when the screening of *Platinum Blonde* had had such a success in Rio de Janeiro that in less than a week all of the beautiful mulatto girls and languid negresses who go out at sunset to walk on the Avenida or to enjoy the coolness of the seashore at Flamingo beach had let down their hair and made themselves up with hot-pink makeup.

On the Beach

"It was so funny!" I concluded. "But unsettling just the same, because they all looked like the reverse of themselves, like those figures we catch sight of against the light when we look at a negative with the naked eye. Imagine this procession of blonde negresses in the light of the sunset, backlit, with the clear hue of their made-up faces and dead but shining hair! They could have been ghosts. One day I even met a black woman who had dyed her hair with henna, which was of a most beautiful Irish red. She was a superb creature, but as a redhead she was royally ridiculous."

"I know," Westmore said to me, in a disenchanted voice. "Very few women know their charm, and even fewer know how to use it to get maximum seductive power by well-balancing all of the gifts of their natural beauty. This is probably due to their lack of knowledge of the most elementary principles of art, architecture, poetry, and . . . makeup. A masterpiece is first and always a work of balance. That is why every pretty girl who wants to make it in the movies should first visit, before I have to bother with her, an architect or a painter from among her friends to teach her the golden rule of symmetry and how it may be that today the most sublime line in a woman is the line of her hair. . . . God, they have no idea, the cuties, and I often feel I'm wasting my time . . ."

"How can you say that?" I said, stupefied by the disillusioned confession that came out of his mouth. "What, you, master? You, the author of the new living models that women all over the world strive to imitate; you, who exercise such an influence through their mediation that the best-known worldly women in the societies of the great cities as well as poor, unknown young girls, lost in the villages of the most far-flung countries, unknowingly obey your decisions or your intentions when they study themselves in their mirrors, when they powder, apply lipstick, make themselves beautiful, and who are altogether ready to sacrifice or modify the most intimate aspects of their personalities according to whatever you might impose upon your daughters, you, the father of the stars . . . "

"Ah, stars!" cried Westmore, "don't talk to me

about stars, they're all gone! There's a crisis, a star crisis . . . here, in Hollywood . . . ask around . . . there's little hope left . . . "

And the great man jumped behind the wheel of his automobile, which had finally arrived, and took off abruptly, spraying passersby with a quadruple shower of dirty water.

The line, I thought to myself as I watched the curve of the spray. He brings life to lines, and curls and shapes and imparts a brilliantined elegance even to the dirty water on the roadway as he charges through it in a skid. What a man! But he's possessed . . .

"What's up with the boss this morning?" asked the kid who had brought Westmore's car. "He's a bit touchy, eh? Would you like a taxi, m'ster?"

"No, kiddo, look — how about a boat!"

As a matter of fact, the rain was coming down twice as hard, and the streets beginning to flood.

THE BIG BREAK: *I'LL STRIKE IT!*

A star crisis in Hollywood? This seems impossible, for you only have to open your eyes to realize that

Hollywood is a nursery of talent bursting with young men and pretty girls.

Youth is everywhere, in the bars, in the boutiques, in the restaurants. The streets are filled with it, and at any hour of the day or night you can watch sensational beauties pass by in cars or find them on foot, in every kind of attire, in shorts, in pajamas, in evening gowns, in raincoats, in furs — but the hair always waved and lustrous — doing their shopping, alone or in pairs, chaperoned by their moms or an old aunt, or followed by a black chauffeur.

In the lounges of the grand hotels where there isn't a vacant room, in the booths of the beauty institutes where they won't take you without an appointment, at the hair salons where you have to stand in line, headstrong budding actresses sit perpetually, unless they're attending one of the courses in gymnastics or rhythmics that are packed from the beginning to the end of the week. Others, marvelously ambitious, faithfully frequent conferences at the Psychic Academy in order to shape their goals, and still others, in order to shape their bodies, frolic in outdoor

Stars at the Market

swimming pools, swim, dive, and practice every kind of sport — horseback riding, skiing, flying, fencing. Contests in beauty or dance are well patronized, and the more or less well known *starlets* and embryonic celebrities count for nothing unless they are found at every sporting event or in the most fashionable hang-outs, dance halls, night spots, casinos, clandestine clubs, races, matches, tennis championships, winter games or sunny beaches — which you can visit on the same day, Sunday — regattas, nighttime celebrations, or aboard *gambling boats* anchored three miles out, or, quite simply, leaving theaters or in a tearoom.

We could also mention just as many young men headed for the cinematic art, many of whom are extremely handsome, all spanking fresh, of a nouveau American chic, sporty and in the know, of eye-pop-ping elegance, in the style of gangsters or, on the con-trary, sober and studied as an English gentleman, or unkempt, as affected as an Oxford bachelor, if not to say a jobless intellectual of 1936. These dandies are found in great numbers, you see them everywhere.

When you've been once or twice to a cocktail

party, when you've heard the innocent laughs of these young people, when you've mingled with them, drunk, laughed, danced, when you've stepped out three or four times with one or the other, when you've scared up the confidences of a girl or chatted with a boy, you're even convinced, it's easy to imagine, that this entire gilded — or so it seems — young generation is destined for the most beautiful future and that nothing is easier than to make it in the movies. Alas! It is nothing of the kind, and among all of these young men not one in a thousand will succeed in making a name on the screen, and not one in ten thousand of these young women will become a star.

Nevertheless, their conversation is crazy with hope. "Just give me one chance," they say, "and I'll break through, *I'll strike it!*" That's their formula.

But there you have it, despite their ferocious resolution, their willpower, their endurance and their courage, despite the money they spend to get here and the privations they undergo, what falls to them by way of bluffing, schemes, and confused plots is in the best case a shadow of a role, a clever walk-on, or, on a rare occasion, to serve as the double for a star — and years pass without fortune smiling on them even once.

What's this all about, given that they're so young, beautiful, active, enthusiastic, and since so many have real talent?

No one has an answer to this, it's a deficiency no one can explain, but the fact is undeniable: *Since the birth of cinema, hardly three or four stars — I can't say how many were originally from Hollywood — have been discovered in Hollywood!*

HOLLYWOOD HODGEPODGE

I had asked for a meeting with Ernst Lubitsch, the great, universally renowned director. I wanted to interview him about the star crisis, since I was particularly curious to have the advice of this capable man on a question of such essential interest for the future of the movies in Hollywood.

It might seem childish to want to offer up a personality as prominent as Ernst Lubitsch; but I beg to make note of the fact that when I asked him for an interview Lubitsch was the director of production at Paramount, and that three days later he had fallen from grace. And yet this man had been responsible for the 60 films that Paramount released from January 1 to December 31, 1935, an output that represents, considering that there are 125 copies of each film, 60 million feet of footage or 18,500 kilometers of finished film, therefore an expenditure, at an average of 5 million francs per film, of at least 300 million francs.

If such a heavy hitter doesn't weigh more than the stroke of a pen in the decisions made without warning by the financial rulers of a cinematic trust, you can easily imagine the superhuman efforts that a newcomer must make to rouse this crushing world and end up breaking into the movies. But this example explains a lot of other things that without it would be incomprehensible; on the one hand, how publicly adored movie stars can disappear from the screen overnight without our ever hearing of them again and without anyone giving them another thought or perhaps telling you what became of them, who was displeased with them and why, and, on the other hand,

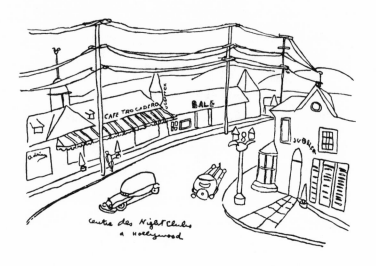

The Nightclub District

how in particular it happens that in the organization of the American cinema the individual counts for zero and even a star is just a gadget.

This dictatorial and, as often as not, anonymous system that operates from top to bottom of the ladder and at every degree in the hierarchy, not only in the studios but in the totality of the social organism of the United States, seems to me one of the most revealing traits of the well-disciplined, conformist, but easily tyrannical mentality of American democracy, which proclaims itself at every turn the champion of free-dom and free will; in any case, this contradiction, which manifests itself even in ordinary life, is the thing in America most irksome to an argumentative Frenchman, willingly irreverent and accustomed to independent judgment and action, above all when it comes to artistic matters concerning direction in the theater or the cinema.

So, my request for a meeting was all the more indiscreet since Lubitsch himself was in trouble and fending for himself. In fact, on the heels of I don't know what circumstances, which no one in Hollywood was able to explain to me clearly but probably for reasons of smoothing out production — the only reasons made available to the public (and for once no one said anything about nepotism in an affair like this!) — the rulers of Paramount decided to halt the shooting of *Hotel Imperial*, the grand picture that Marlene Dietrich was in the midst of filming with Charles Boyer as *leading man* and under the personal supervision of Ernst Lubitsch. Since Marlene was threatening to walk off, refusing to film anything else or work with another director, even talking of quitting Hollywood altogether, you can imagine the contradictory tales and alarming rumors that got going around town; but Hollywood's amazement was taken to a feverish pitch when it was learned, three days later, that Lubitsch had been provisionally replaced by William Le Baron as head of production at Paramount and that he had been granted a three-month leave of absence.

Such was the irrevocable decision, as swift as it was unexpected even for those who thought themselves in the confidences of the gods, that even John

E. Otterson, ex-architect of New York Telephone, who had become by the grace of the bankers Grand Pooh Bah of Paramount, found out without warning.

It was practically a palace revolution, as is frequently sparked in the New Byzantium that is Hollywood, the repercussions of which are unpredictable, for the number of intrigues hatched and unhatched every time, thanks to such an event, can completely upset the *standing* of this or that personality on view, something that always delights heaps of the envious, and this very much to the detriment of all those who make their living in the film industry.

As it happened, Marlene Dietrich quit Paramount to go shoot for Selznick, and a few weeks after her departure, Margaret Sullavan, who needed a great deal of coaxing before accepting to replace her in *Hotel Imperial*, broke her arm, so that the rulers of Paramount found themselves constrained to abandon the idea of making the film, which had already swallowed more than a million dollars, and this poor dear Charles Boyer, who was too exhausted to protest, torn as he was in all directions, left to join Marlene

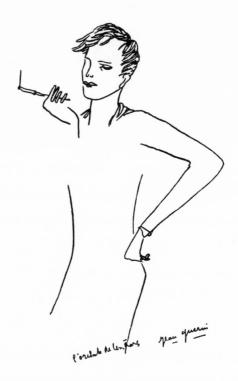

l'oublade de Longchamps   Jean Querni

June Cruze

with Selznick to work with her in *The Garden of Allah*, her next film, which will be released by United Artists. As for Lubitsch, I haven't heard any news of him since I left the Mecca of the Movies; I suppose he won't waste any time before taking some shattering revenge, as is practiced and even required in Hollywood, where, as in China, one must always *save face*. I really believe that here lies the sole tradition of honor in Hollywood.

Naturally, in this hodgepodge, Ernst Lubitsch didn't have the time to oblige me with the desired interview, but this devil of a man, whom Jacques Théry, his friend and most intimate collaborator, says is as spiritual and resourceful as Pagnol and who is surely one of the most levelheaded around, found a way, despite all of the difficulties worrying him, to make known to me his opinion concerning the crisis of the stars.

And herewith is that opinion as I received it by telephone, one night, somewhere around four in the morning. (The voice that spoke to me was alternately tough and inflected, but I attributed the feminine intonations it had at moments, especially at the ends of phrases, to the distance from which it came to me.)

ERNST LUBITSCH'S OPINION

ON THE STAR CRISIS

"The star crisis in Hollywood? . . . But this crisis is real. It is even the only serious crisis we've known here in seven years, in other words since the advent of talkies . . . "

" . . . "

"Today, in 1936, what we most have need of here is neither new screenplays, nor new histories, nor new writers, nor new directors, nor new composers, painters, costumers, set designers, et cetera, but we need new players, new talents, new actors and actresses, for what we lack most here in Hollywood is simply stars, stars of the highest caliber, yes . . . "

" . . . "

"It's urgent, immediate, you'll see! . . . Perhaps never before has so much talent and ingenuity been expended on the screen as in the last seven years. Never have we worked so hard. Never have the photos been so beautiful. Never has lighting been more successfully achieved. The technology is perfect. Sound, voice. Everything is O.K. . . . "

" . . . "

"Yes, today everyone is fine. Everyone is intelligent. Everyone knows how to dress, put on makeup, walk, dance, sing. . . . You say diction still leaves a lot to be desired? . . . but the American public couldn't care a rap, because our girls have never been more stunning than today! . . . "

" . . . "

"It is well-known that all of our actresses have sex appeal and that all of our actors are geniuses. Both are capable of expressing the entire range of human emotion, and we can ask of them anything we'd care to. They are all ready for anything. They are all possessed of an unparalleled docility. Never have they been so well paid. But never have there been fewer names on the poster, names capable of doubling receipts, names capable of packing any theater in the world, names that . . . "

" . . . "

" . . . What's that? . . . You want the names? . . . But I don't want to offend anyone! . . . It's enough for you to know that at the moment, here, in Hollywood, there are only just twenty-three players whose reputation and talent are equal to the expense we are always ready to make on the strength of their name if this name alone can guarantee record receipts! It hardly matters what film it is, so long as one of these twenty-three players appears in the advertising! . . ."

" . . . "

Listen, twenty-three, that's not many, eh? You must admit that this little number is altogether disproportionate to the immense capital that the movie industry risks on it . . . twenty-three stars! . . . yes, not one more! . . . twenty-three . . . "

" . . . "

"Moreover, this number will fade even further by the end of the year: *primo*, because fame, popularity, success are the most ephemeral things there are, and, *secundo*, because among the twenty-three who figure on my list, a few are already in the midst of professional decline . . . "

" . . . "

"Ah! . . . and another thing. . . . The production plan of the English studios for the current year will further impoverish our ranks, already so thin. These days, extremely advantageous offers from British producers attract our stars, our players, and the English shrink from no monetary sacrifice to make them cross the water as fast as possible. It has been said that they are sworn to make all of Hollywood emigrate to Elstree![23] And since, save for two or three exceptions, the English don't have anyone to give us in return, they will deliver us a heavy blow, strike us in a vital organ, it's very grave . . . "

" . . . "

"There is at the moment an Anglo-American rivalry over the stars. We battle it out over a beautiful face in blasts of dollars as if over the possession of an oil field . . . "

" . . . "

"How's that? . . . No, I haven't lost hope, we'll

---

23. Elstree, outside of London, site of the famous British studios.

find a good way to untangle ourselves. As in your country, the D system[24] has always come through for us in America, though the struggle will become more and more heated, it's too serious. . . "

" . . . "

"What? . . . am I ready now to go film in England? . . . Ah, that no, never, I love Hollywood too much, you know! . . . Eh? . . . you'd like to know what I'm going to do if this star crisis goes on and gets worse? . . . Well, you can break the news, I'd rather turn myself into a talent scout than renounce my belief in the conquering beauty of our women and our girls . . . Good night! . . . Hello, hello! . . . what did you say? . . . what's happening to sex appeal in this scuffle? . . . But sex appeal, cher monsieur, is an American invention and the English can whistle for it! If there weren't any more stars, we'd invent something else. . . . Good night! . . . "

---

24. *Système D,* from the word *débrouiller* (to manage to get by or extricate oneself from a difficult situation), is a French colloquialism for finding a way to fix something in a clever, inexpensive, and resourceful manner.

VII

Hollywood
by Night

The Famous Door

AGENTS, HIDDEN MASTERS

OF THE SCREEN

If behind every star there hides a makeup artist, the expert in sex appeal who has bestowed upon her a "certificate of beauty," defined her style, determined her type, who is the real author of that immutable countenance she carries to the screen (it's obvious what has attracted her throng of admirers — more than anything, a *trademark* that gives her commercial value and guarantees her fantastic revenues so long as this name brand, propped up by raving publicity, is popular), to the left and right of every star hover two other men without whom she would never have existed: the agent who launched her, and that star hunter, the *talent scout*, who discovered her.

The agent is the man with a stake in the star while being at the same time on the most intimate terms with the studios, which are no mystery to him, but which he throws into competition by orchestrating behind the scenes press campaigns that excite American public opinion, even shaping it and stealthily managing the good and bad tastes of the crowds.

The agent knows exactly what the public wants from the movies, what the writers are coming up with, what the directors are looking into, what the studios are prepared to pay to take under contract a star they want and whose collaboration they hope to guarantee in their future production. Professionally, it is his duty to know what's happening on every stage and to be aware of every decision made by a firm's executives in the most secret conferences behind closed doors, just as he's got to be on the lookout for any disappointments on a shoot, for faults and weaknesses in a screenplay, for failures, for deficiencies, for the decline of a performer so as to be in position to kick off a reckless war, often a long haul and above all extremely difficult to pull off, for news items, gossip, small talk, pitiless slams, venomous innuendos, vindictive sarcasms, ferocious comparisons, back stabbing, slander, provocation, rivalry, cunning, for the compromise and scandal that precede like an effervescent accompaniment the fall of an old star or the rise of a new one.

The agent must have not only a stockpile of his-and-her replacements on hand and be relentlessly in search of new talent, he has also got to have a magic touch. That's why an agent is always a man of imagination. His head is bursting. He has too many ideas. He's a universal man mixing it up and combing over everything. He's a born imposter, a liar, a schemer. Furthermore, he's a businessman gifted with a flair so prodigious that he can anticipate, foretell the longings of the general public, as well as those of producers, whom he craves to flatter to the point of exhaustion but whom he also exploits thoroughly by stroking them toward his personal views — success requires it. And a good agent is not content just to follow current infatuations, he readily cuts a figure for himself as an innovator by imposing upon everyone a complete unknown he's now launching and who will create a sensation, but whom he will completely tyrannize.

It's an exhausting, desperate occupation, that of

the agent, for to keep on burning candles at both ends he really has to be a gambler at heart and full of devilment, and it is only by means of subtlety, swagger, sleight-of-hand, sheer will, and shrewdness that this enterprising man who spends lavishly ends up slithering and slashing his way into the studios, who never mistrust him so much as when they see him coming after he has finally set his heart on something, caught in the glue, baited, engaged, promised, rigged, seduced, deceived, all the while inspiring trust, living on a grand scale while pursuing some idea in the back of his head, concluded a thousand and one combinations and oblique advances before inflating or dropping the starlet he covets, the one who every time is his new reason to live, his conceit, his pride and joy, his creature, his weakness, his thing, his livelihood, his spiritual daughter, his mistress, his illusion, his chance, his victim, his ruin, the Lady Luck of his dreams — the last or the unknown, who for him, and for a whole world of parasites swarming around him who have complete power over her, will cast unknowingly the fortunes of all.

At the Alabam

TALENT SCOUTS, STAR HUNTERS

So, if the starlet can't do anything in the movies without the intervention of her agent and the agents of her agent, and the film companies can't do without the services of this man and his team of procurers who deliver to them pell-mell stars, men, ideas, scripts, advertising and who shrink from no scandal, the agent, for his part, in order to remain a winner and keep every trump card in hand — the strongest of which is his own personal windfall: a new star — finds himself obliged to mutate into a talent scout, or to have at his service an entire roster of hunters whom he can send out into the countryside and who cost him dearly, these aces, who are this Barnum's Buffalo Bills.

By definition, the talent scout is a simple star hunter. But since he is above all a resourceful type, if he doesn't set up right away as the agent of the star he has just discovered, in other words, if he doesn't thrust himself into the role of his own chief, his own boss, when he thinks he has a white crow in hand, in the manner of the big boss for whom he is supposedly the emissary, he's likely to want to make off with anything that seems to him liable to be of interest, to surprise or please and to make money in the theaters, and not only a beauty or a new talent he has just flushed out, but, since stars seem to be more and more scarce and since he's obliged to make a living, he blindly turns toward Hollywood — and it is because of this that his role is often ill-fated — the greatest possible number of attractions.

So it is that a talent scout will place under contract a black boxer and request that a screenplay be written for him, an acrobatic or baroque dance, an exceptional jazz or extraordinary music hall number, performing animals, a loathsome clown like this unfortunate ballerina Trudi Schoop, nicknamed *The Female Chaplin*, who failed miserably in California, phenomena such as *The Dionne Quintuplets*, the five Canadian sisters who are the stars — you have to wonder what could possibly be the interest in this — of a musical that Fox is in the midst of filming, the hero of some news story, a divorcée or a gangster, a fashionable man or woman who keeps turning up in the newspapers like this poor Cliff Weble, called *The Dandy of New York*, hired for $3,000 a week and who fretted and got bored in Hollywood waiting for a year and a half for his director to come around to remembering him and deign to give him his start, or like Arlette Stavisky, whose coming to the stage they also announced, a girl, a nightclub hostess like Eleanor Powell, the darling of Hollywood who danced twenty-four hours a day and ended up being carried with a nervous breakdown to a mental ward, where she began to shriek, when they put her away, "Charm! . . . darling! . . . let me kill myself! . . . Without dance life is sh - - !" or Mabel Boll, who has no talent whatsoever and isn't pretty, but who has the most beautiful jewelry in America and was the talk of the town for having been mixed up in the incredible adventures of Charles A. Levine, the Don Quixote of transoceanic aviation.

In fact, everything seems good to him, to this hunter of the unseen who no longer knows what saint to devote himself to in order to stand out and distinguish himself, and the more preposterous an idea, the better the chances that he will find it a stroke of genius, for the talent scout is by nature a braggart, but also a gawker, that is to say, a sucker from the big city who ends up allowing himself to believe his own smooth talk — and that's why this kind of person, whatever may be his line, his vulgarity, his allure, his part, his duplicity, his secret troubled and suspicious intentions when he's on the trail of a woman, isn't altogether unsympathetic and why this rogue is in spite of everything a cajoler, disquieting certainly, but plenty popular, picturesque, and naive.

THE FAVORITE HUNTING GROUNDS
OF THE TALENT SCOUT

If the star hunters are a kind of bird of prey, they are among the predatory night birds, for their preferred hunting grounds in every capital in the United States are those feverish islands where, in a riot of light, jazz, multicolored drinks, of cries belched through loudspeakers, of fights, challenges, passions, of endless dances, nocturnal life is in full swing.

In New York, which remains despite the Crash the great center of selection and the principal market where the talent scouts have made their most beautiful finds (95% of all movie stars have debuted on New

At Louis Prima's

York stages), Broadway, the theater district with large, small, and off-street theaters, and then Harlem, with its burlesques, its nightclubs, its dives, its dance halls known around the world.

In Chicago, the famous *Boucle*, "The Loop," with its uninterrupted chain of world fairs, menageries, circuses, bazaars, giant music halls, monster roller-skating rinks, labyrinthine ice rinks, subterranean cabarets full of fake mazes, exhibitionist spectacles livened up with fun-house mirrors, palaces of illusion, Oriental houses, double-exit apartments, clandestine boudoirs.

In New Orleans — home of the last four debutantes invited to try their fortunes or misfortunes in Hollywood and whose names I kept in case we ever hear of them again: Miss Louise Small (18), Miss Wilma Francis (18), Miss Jill Dean (18), and Miss Diana Gibson (20) — the French Quarter with its cafés, its restaurants, its rotisseries, its private dining rooms, its flowered balconies, its red-light streets, its balls, its carnival.

In San Francisco, in the center of the city, the separate districts, *Little Italy* and its shady taverns,

Chinatown and its opium dens, and the most famous poles of attraction on pirate shores — *Barbary Coast*, the *Embarcadero* and the *Marina*, the two best-stocked drug markets in the world; then also, on Saturday night and Sunday, islands, beaches, bayside *Robinson-nades*, a whole immense suburb of nautical celebrations, fireworks, brass bands, fish fries, drunkenness, uproars and songs, with its terraces, its gardens, its groves, its open-air cafés at water's edge, its bridges, its flowered boats, its love kiosks, its drifting ships marked with a single Chinese lantern.

In Miami, swimming pools, gambling houses, floating casinos exploited by Al Capone's gang.

In Galveston, the beauty contest where they choose Miss Universe.

HOLLYWOOD BY NIGHT

Hollywood, too, has no lack of night spots, large and small, but the clients who frequent them are just those people of the cinema who have more or less made it, and if you find a talent scout there it's because he dropped in to relax, to meet with friends or to look up old clients, to chatter, distract himself and not to lie there in wait. As for *Main Street*, which is the hot street, the burning street of Los Angeles, it is lined with penny *cafeterias*, tiny three-cent *chileno* restaurants, nickel cinemas, hourly hotels for a dime, clay-pipe shooting galleries, automated shops, billiard academies, bowling, miniature golf, burlesques and dance halls of the latest kind, pawnshops open all through the night. *Main Street* is the customary promenade of prostitutes and female procurers, of Philippino, Mexican, Asian, and Negro pimps, of sailors on leave from the fleet stationed at San Pedro who go there on binges, and of soldiers out on a spree, but not one Hollywood star, not one debutante would dare to venture there today, and you won't find a single star hunter, unless he's an amateur or among the curious, for what is a night prowler if not at heart a hunter — that is to say, just like a professional talent scout, on the lookout for an encounter, a surprise, a novelty, a sensation?

And as for me, you might have taken me for one of them when, departing in the evening from Nelly's,

Van Vechten's[25] old cook, the heroine of *Paradis des Noirs* who presently owns a tavern at the farthest end of Central Avenue[26] and who forces down you a delicious Southern cuisine, as I extended my nocturnal expedition to Watts, those black encampments scattered in the vague terrain that surrounds Los Angeles and Hollywood which by night are like so many Miracle Courts, and to Wilmington, that den of the Japanese underworld haunted by cheats and smugglers, and which is a veritable blow to the throat, given that in the loud shanties from which peals of laughter

---

25. Carl Van Vechten, 1880–1972. Van Vechten first visited Paris in the late 1800s and maintained close ties with French and American expatriate writers. A lifelong interest in African-American culture (Van Vechten had many prominent black friends) culminated in his 1926 novel, *Paradis des Noirs* (Nigger Heaven), the ironic title of which refers both to the uppermost theater gallery where blacks were often forced to sit and consequently to the geographical location of Harlem relative to Manhattan. As the author of *Anthologie nègre* (1921) and a major catalyst in the early French avant-garde interest in African culture, Cendrars knew the book well, and perhaps also knew Van Vechten's *Spider Boy*, a light satire of Hollywood culture published in 1927. See Edward Lueders, *Carl Van Vechten* (New York: Twayne Publishers, 1965).

26. Central Avenue in South Central Los Angeles, well into the 1950s one of the liveliest jazz scenes outside of Harlem.

spread, both men and women smoke *marijuana*, the famous laughing plant of the ancient sect of flagellants, Los Hermanos de Sangre de Cristo, whose penances are appalling and who down to this day celebrate from time to time a "blood crucifixion," like the one that took place on February 5, 1936, in Morada, New Mexico, which was the date of the last known crucifixion . . . before the 80 civilians crucified and burned alive by the Frente Popular[27] in Almendralejo, Spain, at the end of August 1936 . . .

But that is another story, a true story, and not from the movies.

---

27. Popular Front, the coalition of Socialists, Communists, and workers' parties that came to power in February 1936 and was overthrown by a military counterrevolution in July 1936, marking the beginning of the Spanish Civil War.

Departure (aboard the *Wisconsin*)

*San Pedro, Champerico, San José-de-Guatémala, Acajutla, La
Libertad, La Union, Corinto, Punta Arenas, Cristobal, Saint
Thomas* (Virgin Islands), *Corvo* (The Azores), *Le Havre*
February 17 to March 19, 1936

 F I N

DESIGN / COMPOSITION   Jacqueline Gallagher-Lange

TEXT FACE   Cochin 11.5 / 20

DISPLAY FACE   Bernhard Modern

PRINTING / BINDERY   Edwards Brothers, Inc.